It Was Never About Justice

"We've all been through challenges and tragedy in our lives and reading Mike describe all that happened to him is heart wrenching. But in the midst of it all, It is easy to hear Jesus' voice in his words. It's a calming voice of the One who says, 'Don't worry,' 'Have courage,' and 'Trust in Me.' *It Was Never About Justice* will help you understand that Jesus is the only true source of peace no matter what you are facing".

Megan Alexander
Host *Inside Edition*, Author, Mom of 3

"When you read *It Was Never About Justice*, you will realize true freedom, even in prison. For most of us, a prison is a place of no hope. But this book is evidence that God is our hope and will always be with us where ever we are and does His work through us."

Joseph Admassu
Suffolk, VA

"*It Was Never About Justice* shows us how the world's flawed concept of justice is subordinate to God's divine plan. For those victims of injustice, this book is a clarion call to stand firm and watch God turn what was meant for evil into abounding good. It is not simply a compelling story about a difficult experience. It is the chronicling of a transforming encounter with the One who redeems and restores in the darkest of times."

Michael Hartsfield, Ph.D, President
Aileron Private Client Services

IT WAS NEVER ABOUT JUSTICE

EXPOSING CORRUPTION, REVEALING GRACE

MICHAEL MORISI

NEW YORK

LONDON • NASHVILLE • MELBOURNE • VANCOUVER

IT WAS NEVER ABOUT JUSTICE

Exposing Corruption, Revealing Grace

Published in New York, New York, by Morgan James Publishing. Morgan James is a trademark of Morgan James, LLC. www.MorganJamesPublishing.com

Unless marked otherwise, Scripture taken from THE HOLY BIBLE, NEW INTERNATIONAL VERSION® (NIV) Copyright© 1973, 1978, 1984, 2011 by Biblica, Inc.™. Used by permission of Zondervan.

Scriptures marked ESV are taken from THE HOLY BIBLE, ENGLISH STANDARD VERSION® (ESV) Copyright© 2001 by Crossway, a publishing ministry of Good News Publishers. Used by permission.

Proudly distributed by Ingram Publisher Services.

A FREE ebook edition is available for you or a friend with the purchase of this print book.

CLEARLY SIGN YOUR NAME ABOVE

Instructions to claim your free ebook edition:
1. Visit MorganJamesBOGO.com
2. Sign your name CLEARLY in the space above
3. Complete the form and submit a photo of this entire page
4. You or your friend can download the ebook to your preferred device

ISBN 9781636981215 paperback
ISBN 9781636981222 ebook
Library of Congress Control Number: 2022952104

Cover and Interior Design by:
Chris Treccani
www.3dogcreative.net

Morgan James is a proud partner of Habitat for Humanity Peninsula and Greater Williamsburg. Partners in building since 2006.

Get involved today! Visit: www.morgan-james-publishing.com/giving-back

To every man and woman in the United States who has been targeted, falsely accused, and prosecuted by the federal justice system for crimes that cannot be prosecuted at the state level because they are not violations of the law.

To everyone serving long terms for minor crimes in the federal facilities where the conditions would make it illegal to house human beings anywhere else in the country.

Finally, to everyone who has suffered any kind of pain, disappointment, and sadness who didn't know they could find peace in the midst of that pain through a relationship with Jesus Christ.

Table of Contents

Author's Note

It Was Never about Justice, a memoir of sorts, depicts actual events in my life as honestly as my recollection permits. While all persons within are actual individuals, names and identifying characteristics have been changed or omitted to respect their privacy. I am sure I will be "corrected" on some points, mostly of the "he said-she-said "kind. While this is a book of memory, and memory has its own story to tell, I used letters and journals to help me and have done my best to make it tell a truthful story and hope some good, perhaps even some change, comes of it.

Introduction

Before you read this book, a memoir, let me introduce myself to you. It is important you know me and my character because this was written not only to present truths you might find hard to believe about how our federal justice system works and how the Federal Bureau of Prisons functions, but also to assure you our God is sovereign and directs every step of your life to accomplish His will and plan for you. Sometimes, we think things go badly for us because God let them happen, but in reality, there are times God sends us into situations because we told Him we would go anywhere He needed us, and if we are faithful and trust Him, those bad situations will turn out good and for His glory. It is easy for us to believe that when things are going well, but it's often difficult when things don't go the way we planned or hoped.

I met Jesus in 1995. I had been a Christian for my whole life, raised in the Church. However, I was a Christian only in name, certainly not in behavior. In 1995, I was the Security Manager for the Founders Inn & Conference Center, which is a part of Christian Broadcast Network (CBN)/Regent University, and it was there some men led me to a real revelation of who

Jesus is and who I was in His eyes. From that day, I pursued the Lord with all my heart, and while far from perfect and had a lot to learn about walking with Him, I did my best. And He was always right there to pick me up when I fell.

In 2011, I was working for a government contractor that provided security solutions for several of the nation's most protected facilities as the senior business development manager. My wife and I had four boys, two grown and two babies. My work took me away from home nearly every week, but we made the sacrifice because the work was stable. I loved what I was doing, and we were building our future.

In a moment I can only compare to Jerry Maguire's famous scene in the movie by the same name, when he woke up in the middle of the night and wrote the document that got him fired but launched his new business, I decided it was time to start a new airline in America. I know it sounds crazy—to one day decide to start an airline—and believe me, I thought it was too. But after lots of prayer and conversations with friends who knew the industry well, I went for it. My primary thought as I searched for a team of experienced leaders for various areas of the operation was they had to be lovers of Christ, above all else. I was determined to launch a large commercial business led by people who lived their lives according to the values and principles of Jesus. God brought the right team together, and we were on our way.

We worked hard, traveling the country and talking to those capable of funding this operation, which would take millions of dollars to get off the ground. In every meeting with prospective investors, they said the same thing: "I trust you. I believe in the plan and am investing in you, Mike." I took that seriously and committed myself to protecting their investments and being a good steward of God's provision.

After several years of planning, we were finally in the air. You will hear more of this story later. What I want you to know about me before you get into this book is, in my life, God comes above all else, followed by my wife, then our children, and then work. As Scripture directs, I worked as if working for Him only, to please Him and bring Him glory. Life was good, and I trusted this major life move was ordained by Him and that He would walk through it with us every step of the way.

Well, things didn't go as planned, at least not according to my plan for the airline. You'll read more about that as well. In the midst of this launch, I lost one of my sons in 2012, which devastated me and took me away from God for a time. Then, in 2015, after we stopped flying, I heard the call of God again to move on and work directly for Him. Two days after that call, someone I had met only once asked me if I would join a ministry working to get US congressional representatives to establish prayer caucuses across the country and commit to praying before making decisions for our nation.

I accepted and spent a year with them, meeting some of the greatest men and women of faith I've ever known. Many remain friends today. I saw powerful men and women pour out their love for Jesus in ways that gave me hope for our country.

I tell you this backstory so as you read my story, you might avoid the temptation to question the validity of some of what I'll share. Some of it is shocking, but every word is, indeed, true.

These facts might help you understand what is happening in our country:

The United States has the highest incarceration rate worldwide and houses the largest number of prisoners worldwide. Roughly 2.12 million people were incarcerated in the US in 2020. The United States has less than 5 percent of the world's population, yet we have almost 20 percent of the world's total prison population. Let me repeat that: though only 5 percent of the world's population lives in the United States, it is home to 20 percent of the world's prison population. Not only does the current overpopulated, under-funded system hurt those incarcerated, but it also digs deeper into the pockets of taxpaying Americans. The recidivism rate is above 70 percent, which points to the notion that not only are we imprisoning more people than any other country, our prison system is doing nothing to help rehabilitate these men and women to give them a chance for success when they are released [paraphrased and summarized].[1]

As if that were not enough, charges of prosecutorial misconduct against federal prosecutors are on the rise. The primary types of misconduct are 1.) failure to disclose exculpatory evidence, 2.) introducing false evidence, 3.) using improper arguments, and 4.) discriminating jury selection. You will learn as you read, these are all much more commonplace than you think, certainly not hidden well, and rarely punished when discovered. Because prosecutors climb the ladder based on wins, the need to win takes precedence over justice. A high-profile case gets them even more accolades.

Finally, keep in mind the definition of justice that I've used for this book (from various dictionaries): "The quality of being just; righteousness, equitableness, or moral rightness . . . to uphold the justice of a cause; rightfulness or lawfulness, as of a claim or title; justness of ground or reason: to complain with justice. The moral principle determining just conduct." Throughout my memoir, you will read about our "justice" system and perhaps realize it does not match many of those definitions.

The Federal Bureau of Prisons is charged with protecting society by confining offenders in prisons and community-based facilities that are safe, humane, cost-efficient, and appropriately secure and by providing inmates with programs and services to assist them in becoming proactive law-abiding citizens when they return to their communities. I propose that what they actually do is paramount to slavery and abuse.

1

THE LETTER

---

*"For my thoughts are not your thoughts, neither
are your ways my ways," declares the Lord. "As the
heavens are higher than the earth, so are my ways
higher than your ways and my thoughts than your
thoughts."* (Isaiah 55:8)

2019

There is a sick feeling that hits your spirit and stomach when
you see a letter addressed to you from the US Attorney's
Office. I had just returned from China where I preached
the gospel to those who could be incarcerated just for listening.
Their faith and willingness to give up everything for God was
profound. I believe God gives us moments in life where we

absolutely know He is with us and has a plan for us, and this was one of those times for me.

I was supposed to go to China to fall even deeper in love with Him. I thought it was so I could return to minister more often or with increased fervor, but He had other plans. Two weeks after returning, after a peaceful Friday at work, I arrived home to my family with plans for pizza and a movie night. My family loved Fridays, times when we watched movies or played games and just enjoyed being together. My boys were just ten and twelve, and my wife was my best friend, someone who always pointed our family to Jesus.

I had no idea this letter from the US Attorney's Office was coming, and as I read it, I couldn't imagine how they could believe I had done what they were accusing me of doing. It is not in my nature to break the law; I am a rule follower. I even worked in law enforcement for many years and believed in our system of justice. The content of the letter—the accusations—had to be an error.

"You are a target in a criminal investigation into wire fraud, money laundering and tax evasion." I laughed out loud when I read those words because I was sure they had made a mistake. I called our former corporate attorney, who assured me there was no way I or anyone had done anything that would warrant those charges. He thought they were fishing. What neither he nor I knew was that regardless if we handled everything in accordance with the law, if they (government officials) wanted to paint a different picture, if they targeted you, they have the resources and power to do so.

My mind raced with all of the stories I had heard of good people being targeted by over-zealous government prosecutors, eager to get exposure for handling high-profile cases. I wondered what I could and would do against that kind of power. How would it impact my family? This would equally hurt my wife and kids if it continued.

All I could do, as I held the letter with shaking hands, was pray that God would intervene and not let this happen to us.

The issue is, the federal government has a statute called "scheme to defraud," and it gives a prosecutor the power to target an individual for behaviors considered legal and call them a *scheme* to commit a crime.

According to the law, in order to make a wire fraud conviction, the prosecution must prove that you were part of a scheme to defraud another person or party. In other words, you planned to use a false statement, promise, or misrepresentation in order obtain money or something of value from someone else. I was charged with sending emails to unsecured creditors letting them know we did not have funds to repay them which was the truth because all funds we did have had to be used for secured and superior debt according to bankruptcy laws. At the time I sent the emails, it was directed by the CEO and in-house Counsel because I had the relationships. I was not employed by the company and had no authority to determine how the funds were dispersed nor was I authorized signer on the bank account but believed and still believe all bankruptcy laws were followed.

If it cannot be proven that you acted knowingly or with the specific intent to defraud someone else, you cannot be convicted of wire fraud. Participation in a wire fraud scheme is not enough to secure a conviction alone, you need to have known about the scheme and participated in it with the goal of deceptively obtaining money or valuables from someone else.

This incredibly vague law remains on the books for prosecutors to use to accomplish their mission—a mission that may include punishing, not real criminals with intent to commit crimes, but people who are convenient to target, everyday people who give them the high-profile cases they need to help them advance their careers.

To give you some perspective, let's go back five years to when a company I had launched ceased operations, back to when we dissolved my airline.

2014

The day we ceased service at PEOPLExpress Airlines was a difficult day for all of us, especially for me. I had launched the airline after a night of reflection about my life and where my passions lay. Having worked nearly ten years in the airline industry in a senior leadership position, I had a good understanding of airline operations and believed the timing was perfect for a new airline that would make fair pricing and excellent customer service priorities. I was blessed with an incredible team of wonderful professionals who shared my passion to not only launch a new commercial passenger airline, but to do it with character and integrity.

And we did that. No matter what you may have heard or read in the papers, I think by now, we all know how trustworthy the "news" is. Even the government news sites posted information about my charges that were blatantly untrue, one, the DOJ Office of Inspector General claiming I was charged with misappropriation of State and Federal funds from the Small Community Air Service Development Program, which I had no control over nor was charged with. The lengths they will go to try to discredit a target in the news is an example of how far the justice system has fallen from real justice.

The team of senior leaders I selected had a couple of things in common: they were passionate about the industry and well-experienced, and they lived their lives as followers of Christ, following His example and model His standards of truth and honesty.

We successfully launched in June 2014 and operated for several months with results well above our projections. People Express Airlines (as we were commonly named) was a dream come true. Our success far exceeded any forecasts we had developed. The public loved the direct routes, the low fares, and especially the exceptional customer service. We had completed all of the filing requirements for a large public offering and were well on our way to expanding and posting our first profit less than a year into operations. It was funny to hear all of the airline analysts—these top-notch, self-proclaimed professionals—say we wouldn't last, but our sales and the almost viral following we created were overwhelmingly positive.

One example of our culture was if someone checked in for a flight at People Express and communicated they were experiencing any tragedy or struggle in their life, most times, the customer service manager stopped what they were doing and offered to pray with that passenger. Before many of our flights, you would see small groups of people in the boarding area, huddled and praying. It was not uncommon for one or more members of our staff to be in that huddle, praying with them. At one point, a local news station covering our operations on a stormy night poked fun at this, and the public response on social media made them regret it. It was beautiful—something we should see more of in the marketplace. People caring for each other and praying for those in need. We were unashamed of our faith in God.

Our initial investors were thrilled with our operating results. By September, we had advance sales heading into the holidays that put us on track to earn an operating profit in our sixth month of operation, something never done before by any airline. We were negotiating for a third aircraft and had a large public/private offering scheduled for early October 2014 to raise $25–30 million to get us to the next phase of growth. New York bankers were optimistic about this offering. Then, while I was in New Orleans, celebrating the launch of our newest route, I received a call I never expected, right before taking the stage at a business luncheon to announce our plans for their city.

A twenty-year-old working for a contractor on the ramp had driven a service truck into the side of one of our Boeing 737 aircraft while passengers were already loaded, about to head to West Palm Beach, damaging the plane and grounding it indefinitely. The damage was significant and would require work at an FAA-approved maintenance center followed by inspections before being cleared for passenger flights again. This was going to take more than a few weeks to repair. To get a backup aircraft, we needed help from one of the other scheduled airlines that had FAA scheduled operating authority , and, as you can imagine, none wanted to help an upstart carrier fill planes as they headed to a public offering.

We operated only two aircraft with busy schedules and could not have anticipated losing one of them. At one point, we received permission from a regional FAA director to use an experienced charter carrier , Orange Air from Orlando to fly our scheduled routes. He had decided for the good of the public we could do this. We contracted with the charter company, had one of their planes flown in on a Saturday morning, loaded it with passengers, and were ready to go. We believed the crisis had been averted, and we would make it through this.

Then came the call just as the Captain activated his fight plan. The senior director of the FAA had received an urgent complaint from another scheduled carrier about us being permitted to use a charter carrier, and the approval was withdrawn. This political move had devastating consequences for our business and the hundreds of our passengers whose flights were canceled. Looking back, had this one decision been handled with the best interest of the public in mind, rather than a government official deciding to satisfy one carrier who didn't want to see us succeed, I believe we would still be flying today.

We did a pretty creative job of flying our routes with one plane for a few days. We also purchased flights for hundreds of customers on other carriers. We knew we couldn't maintain this schedule for long. Then, on one stormy morning, after a bird strike into one of our engines, an inspection revealed the engine would need to be replaced. That would cost close to $1 million and take over a week to handle.

We were done.

In late September 2014, we ceased operations. There were many tears in our offices. We had a team of nearly 200 individuals nationwide who loved what they did and loved the company we had built together. We had worked tirelessly to keep flying, but the public didn't know what had gone on behind closed doors. All they would hear about in the news were the stranded customers and angry people having to pay double what they had paid us to fly home on different carriers. While other carriers were gouging our customers with fares that were double or triple what they had paid us, only Delta Airlines honored our fares and handled our customers with exemplary customer service. We will always have a special place in our hearts for the leadership at Delta.

The planned public offering was suspended by the Securities Exchange Commission because of the significant change in our status. Our CEO furloughed the entire staff except for himself and our in-house counsel. Most of our senior leadership team continued to meet, refusing to accept we were done, and a few of us still tried to find funding to get back in the air. Nonetheless, we all knew, if we had to close permanently, we would handle it with the same integrity with which we had operated with from the start.

We were very close . . . we had negotiated an acquisition with the charter carrier we had tried to use and were going to use funds we were expecting from a $550,000 refund from the New York Airport Authority to pay them to get their three planes flying for us out of Newport News, Virginia. However, at the eleventh hour, because of a strained relationship with the airport director, he advised Towne Bank to seize those funds as soon as they hit our account. They did and then applied the $550,000 to the balance of a loan we had obtained, which was guaranteed by the airport. They did this even though we were not in default.

As part of our launch, Towne Bank (a local, hometown bank) had granted us a $5 million loan, secured by the Newport News Airport Authority. These funds were offered by the airport to speed up our launch date. We had originally scheduled an October 2014 launch, but the airport wanted to capitalize on the busy summer season and receive an FAA grant, one offered to them if the airport established New York and Boston service before June 30, 2014. The airport offered the loan to help us fly four months sooner than planned. I was not in favor of using this loan to fly sooner than we were ready but I had little ability to influence the decision at this point. We needed more than $5 million to successfully launch and sustain through the early months, and I had in my mind a minimum of $12 million. We accepted this loan because of a commitment from a group of investors from Atlantic City who pledged $15 million to be invested as part of a larger real estate deal by mid to late summer 2014, but I had concerns about this group's ability to close their deal.

They never came through.

When money is involved, trust goes out the window and friends forget their friendships. I guess, at times, it is warranted, but in this case, we all wanted the same thing, to see People Express flying and successful. Millions of investment dollars disappeared over a bad attitude and someone's unprofessionalism. Even as I write this, it breaks my heart to think about it.

By November 2014, the CEO, chief counsel, CFO, and I were working together to bring this dream come true to an end and do it as smoothly as possible. Our chief counsel directed every move to ensure compliance with bankruptcy laws, under the direction of the CEO, and I acted as an advisor to them, primarily because I had established almost all of the company relationships with vendors and investors. These people had been communicating with me for years, so they only knew me. One instruction I was given by the chief counsel was to respond to all requests from unsecured vendors by telling them we did not have the funds to pay them (because bankruptcy laws required that the funds we did have be used for taxes and priority debts first). We made it clear that if we could get funded to restart the company, they would be made whole.

It was these emails that would come back to haunt me later. These *legal* emails, sent to unsecured creditors and that complied with bankruptcy law, are what the prosecutors would later call "a scheme to defraud." We had carefully calculated the funds we expected to come in from insurance claims and refunded deposits and knew we could pay all of the company tax debt and cover some of the secured debt with the airport and a portion of the accrued/unpaid payroll to officers, some who had worked for up to fourteen months without pay over the previous three years. This payout plan was approved by the company's board of directors and by our largest investor, who represented a group that had invested over $2 million. We did not arrive at these decisions without the full agreement of all parties involved.

That's the red flag that got the government's attention—paying accrued salaries to officers. However, it was a legitimate company debt, and the law says those are priority debts and must be paid. Most of us were owed well over $120,000 each. Additionally, we had all invested personal funds alongside other investors to get us flying. Even as we questioned it, the board and our investors agreed we should use the funds to pay those salaries. In the end, we all received less than half of what we were owed.

The CEO finished closing People Express by December 2015. It was another sad day. I moved on, taking a position with a national ministry in January 2015, and felt the Lord's call for me to serve Him in this role, but it still hurt to see this amazing dream come to an end. But God knew what He was doing, and life moved on.

Five years later, I stood alone in my room, reading that letter, which in no way described anything that happened, and I felt stranded in unfamiliar territory. Thoughts of the stories of others being targeted and charged with ridiculous crimes pummeled my brain. I immediately knelt in prayer, asking God to reveal this for what I already believed it was . . . a fishing expedition with no basis at all for any legal claim. I called our former in-house counsel, and he assured me it was nothing more than that because we had done everything according to the law. I felt relieved but braced myself for what the government might be up to.

2

BREAKING NEWS

For the righteous will never be moved; he will be remembered forever. He is not afraid of bad news; his heart is firm, trusting in the Lord (John 16:33, ESV).

2017

On an otherwise ordinary day, a news report revealed the airport had covered $4.5 million of the loan balance we defaulted on in 2014. A disgruntled former tenant of the airport had a conflict with the airport director and got revenge by telling the media about this loan. It came as a shock to the state, and the news report indicated the airport director had allegedly withheld reporting to the state that he had used their funds to repay the loan. I do not know what the airport director had reported or what the disgruntled tenant knew, but this news

report caused a major investigation by state and federal authorities, who wanted to know how the loan was made and how the
money was spent.

In my first and only meeting with the large team of investigators, I learned they were concerned about what People
Express Airlines had done with the money and if there had been
some deal to pay some of those funds to the airport director or
other leaders in Newport News. About ten investigators and I
gathered around a table, and I answered their questions to the
best of my ability; however, it became quickly apparent that
I had limited knowledge about the specific details of how the
loan was obtained or about the authority to release bank records.
And I couldn't provide any of the documentation they needed.
It wasn't my role in the company. I arranged for them to gain
access to everything they needed from the company's CFO.

After several months, I heard from the lead investigator that
the leadership team from People Express was no longer a target
of the government's investigation, and they had accounted for
every dollar we spent of the state-guaranteed loan. We knew
this would be the outcome because we had been careful to handle our finances with integrity. Despite this truth, several news
articles and even federal agencies would manipulate the facts
over the next few weeks, months, and years to imply the money
was spent too quickly and was unaccounted for. Even an editor
at the Daily Press newspaper, who did his own calculations—
with no experience or training in airline start-up expenses or
budgeting—determined and published that nearly $2 million
was unaccounted for, an outright lie. I know it comes as no
surprise that a newspaper printed something completely false to

sell more papers, but that is what happened. Always be careful what news sources you trust.

In fact, none of those who offered their public *opinions* ever launched an airline and had done little to no research into the costs involved. But facts and truth aren't often the driving forces behind news reports. I guess in today's media world, the truth doesn't sell.

Nearly a year after these meetings, in August 2018, I was asked to come to the federal building downtown to meet with IRS criminal investigators about People Express. Against my better judgment, I went alone and made it clear to them I was not an officer of the company in November 2014, did not sign on the new bank account opened by the CEO, and had no authority to move money from the account they were questioning me about—facts they already knew. It was disturbing how the entire interview unfolded. Based on this experience, I would strongly suggest no one ever goes, even when invited by federal investigators, in for "a talk," especially with the IRS. They answer to no one, and there is little to no appeal process once they decide you did something wrong. And they don't need any evidence to support their claims. In my experience, they have one mission: to get you to say something that isn't completely true or twist your words to give them something they can say to a jury to make you look guilty. That's it. After all, they already know the answers to every question they ask.

In this meeting, the investigator would make these ridiculous statements, and I would tell him he was incorrect and provide the truth, but he would simply move on, offering no acknowledgment of my statement, even though he was headed in the wrong direction and assuming incorrect things.

I soon realized he wasn't looking for the truth. He was building a case and had no concern for truth or facts because they disputed what he needed to accomplish his task, which was to lay blame on someone—anyone—over this failed airline money. There was no way they were going to indict the senior political representative/airport authority leader/bank officer, the city manager, the airport, or the legal team of attorneys who orchestrated the loan and assured everyone it was lawful. They weren't going to go after the eighty-year-old former CEO, who directed the spending of every dime during our shut down. No, they were going after the high-profile former founder and president of the airline, the one who was a pastor and had worked in ministry for the past five years.

Once they realized nothing was mishandled at the company, the investigator then told me he felt I had under-reported my income for several years. He made allegations that the company had issued me checks that were not reported on my W-2 form. I explained to him the only payments he could have seen from the company were reimbursements for business expenses I had paid with my personal credit cards. Surely, I was not the first businessperson with reimbursable business expenses, especially with a start-up. We had documented every dime, but he didn't care.

Again, I believe the prosecutors used this tactic to discredit their target: me. I was certain I had reported every dollar of income. He admitted he came to his conclusion by adding every deposit made into my personal checking account and assumed it was all income. Wow! He never accounted for gifts, money provided by my family during the times without pay, the reimbursed business expenses paid with my personal credit card, and more. It felt more like they were trying to find something but couldn't, so they created a way to make it look like I had done something wrong.

It's a terrible and unethical strategy, making a target look so bad that the public—and especially a future jury—simply believes the individual is guilty. Their mission was to destroy any credibility I had by making it seem like I intentionally did things wrong (i.e., unlawfully) but that I presented myself as someone who had integrity.

Don't take my word for it. Later, my public defender admitted this as truth. She detailed exactly how federal prosecutors work, especially when they have a weak case. They spend six months leading up to trial finding anyone they can to say what they need them to say on the stand to discredit the defendant. For them it is not about trying to use facts to prove someone broke the law, just as long as they can make the jury so sure I am guilty because I can't be trusted, by the time I testify they aren't even really listening. I felt shame for the manner in which our government, the institution I had trusted for my whole life, could be so manipulative in achieving some fabricated agenda of their own creation.

Worse, this investigator had the audacity to tell me we shared the same faith. *No, my friend, we don't . . . because in my faith, there is no way I would abuse my power to hurt an innocent man.*

And, friends, I am not the only one this has happened to . . . or is happening to, every day.

I left the meeting comfortable with the knowledge I had done nothing wrong but felt concerned because of how I was treated. The authorities made it clear: if they believe I under-reported my income, it was *my job* to prove otherwise, even though the documentation already had. My point is, innocent until proven guilty isn't the case when you become the target of the IRS.

Afterward, I made several requests to the lead investigator for the information he had promised to send me so I could address the deposits, but he never followed up, never provided me any evidence to support his conclusions. He sent all of his revised calculations to the IRS, which subsequently added them to my income and assessed their penalties, with interest on new tax debt, all with no communication with me. I find this process corrupt and sickening, and there must be some controls put in place to prevent this from happening because I am certain that I am not the only victim.

This story, my story, should concern all Americans, given today, in September 2022, the Biden Administration has a hiring plan for 87,000 new agents, who will all have one agenda—to audit as many people as possible to find discrepancies, even, as in my case, if they have to create those discrepancies out of nothing.

2019

Life had moved on. I was working in ministry, traveling quite a bit, preaching, and leading a ministry that had grown across the nation. In March, I went on a trip to China with two pastors to preach the gospel and came back even more in love with Jesus than ever before. I saw a genuine faith in the people of China, a faith that had them willing to give up everything to love and serve the Lord. All at significant risk.

About a week later, that letter from the US Attorney's Office arrived in my mailbox. What I had feared the most about how our government was operating within the "justice" system came to fruition and crashed into my life in a way I never could have expected.

Before going forward, I want to make something clear: I believe there are hundreds of judges, prosecutors, public defenders, investigators, and others in the federal system that are honest people, looking for the truth, punishing guilty people for crimes they did commit, and we need those people. There are, however, some who crave power so much, they will build high-profile cases out of nothing, manipulate facts to suit their needs, create evidence where none exists, hide exculpatory evidence, then use intimidation tactics to punish people when they don't go along with their schemes. If you google the number of federal prosecutors who have committed acts of fraud and prosecutorial misconduct, you will see hundreds listed and most are still working in their position. I have to wonder how high this abuse of power goes. Do judges know this is happening? Are there behind-closed-door conversations, where prosecutors, public defenders and judges determine the outcome of a trial or sentencing before the defendant and their attorney ever walk into the courtroom? I believe the relationship between federal public defenders and prosecutors is incestuous, and it must change or fair representation will never happen.

As I scoured the full letter, I read that if I called within ten days and came in to meet with them, we could resolve it without an indictment. So I called. And called and called. No live person ever picked up the phone. There was no response. I had a friend, a local attorney, who called for me and was told the offer to come in no longer applied because the prosecutor had decided the case was too high-profile and it needed to be handled publicly and through the courts. *Publicly?* That was my confirmation; there was an alternate agenda here.

The following week, the airport director was indicted on a dozen charges relating to the guarantee of the loan using state funds and some other inappropriate uses of airport money for personal use. I was surprised by the news because I knew corporate counsel had vetted the loan—both in-house and through outside counsel—and the airport chief counsel and the bank's counsel agreed it was a legal use of airport funds based on the wording in Virginia law. Additionally, the airport board reviewed the proposal and also approved it, so I wondered why the airport director was being charged. My only answer is that they couldn't charge the leadership of the airport board, or the airport attorney, or the many other Newport News powerbrokers who were involved in this.

Rumor around Newport News was the local bank and airport attorney had to repay the bulk of the loan. It seemed to me this made it clear; they had done wrong. But the government only went after the airport director and a former airline founder (me). I guess we were easy targets.

The next surprise was how the government worded their claims about how the director and I got this loan and spent it all in a month, painting a devastating picture that would soon develop more clearly. And very little of the picture was factual.

3

INDICTMENT

The heart is deceitful above all things and beyond cure.
Who can understand it?
"I the Lord search the heart and examine the mind,
to reward each person according to their conduct,
according to what their deeds deserve" (Jeremiah
17:9–10).

2019

On May 19, I was ordained as a pastor at a beautiful cere-
mony with my family and friends. It was a humbling experience to know God had called me into this work, and I had
fulfilled His plan for me to study and learn about Him and be
considered prepared for this honor. I was thrilled and couldn't
wait to see all God had for me.

That night, I proudly told Him I was His, and He could send me wherever He needed me to go. I was hoping it would be back to China for a season. I was not prepared for the call I received the following day. It was from the federal investigator, telling me I had been indicted, and he was giving me a chance to turn myself in the next morning by 9:00 a.m. He told me the usual procedure was to bring a team in the middle of the night to arrest me, but "he was doing me a favor." It would have been almost funny if it wasn't so sick. We have all seen the instances of abuse of power the government law enforcement agencies have used, sending huge teams of heavily armed personnel to the homes of people indicted on low-level, white-collar crimes, people with no criminal or violent history at all.

I fell on my knees before God and cried out because I could not believe this was happening to me. There was no way I—or anyone at People Express—had done anything wrong. We were certain of it. I realized this ordeal would require me to surrender to His will, just as I had promised, and be still as we awaited what He had planned.

Now this debacle would go public, spread like fire in the newspapers and in local news reports, and my entire family would suffer as a result. The injustice angered me, and I thought, *I must fight this*. What would come next was so shocking, it became frightening.

I surrendered on Tuesday morning, as promised, and after spending six hours in a holding cell, I was released—with conditions. They were the ones you'd expect: be of good behavior, don't leave the state, and others. But they added I could have no contact with the former CEO or CFO of People Express, no contact with the media, and could not discuss the case on social media or anywhere else with anyone other than counsel. Of course, the government gets to publish dozens of articles in the news with their angle on the story, "news" supported not by facts, but by an agenda. They ensured their side got out long before I could talk about what really happened. This is not justice by any means. It is corrupt and manipulative. The government can and will drag your name through the mud. Dozens of news agencies use the ridiculous claims of the government and exaggerate them for effect, and they both spread them. However, I, as the accused, may not respond. If I violate those conditions, I go to a local jail cell until my trial, which effectively stops me from communicating with anyone.

These governmental agencies, investigators, and prosecutors don't even try to hide the power they wield. In my case, they knew if I started talking about the truth of this case, then the jury pool may get to hear not just their contrived side, but both sides of the story. It became clear right away that they wanted to control the narrative, and it was theirs to create and control as they saw fit. Some of the press releases they wrote made blatantly false claims about me. Imagine reading lies about yourself and then being ordered not to respond. My credibility was burned in the spreading firestorm before I had a chance to yell, "Foul!" And...my faith was tested.

Here, I want to summarize the charges against me from my point of view. I wrote five emails to unsecured creditors. These emails explained we did not have the money to pay them. We had funds in our account, but those funds were legally bound for tax debt and priority debts and could not be paid to those creditors, according to the law. The law that would later not matter to the government. In fact, our counsel and board cautioned us *not* to pay anything to any of those unsecured creditors, or, they said, we would violate bankruptcy law. The government decided that sending those emails constituted fraud because there *were* funds in the bank, available to use *or not,* and as a result, each instance of fraud also meant the money we had used for other legal purposes was illegal, so they threw in money laundering for good measure.

Remember that term "scheme to commit fraud law" they use? Then the tax charges were piled on top because my deposits didn't match my income so, altogether, I was facing eighteen felonies. I believe the law has been structured to give them the ability to do this so juries and the public immediately believe the government's charges because they are so numerous. You must be guilty if there are eighteen charges, right? And that is exactly how it happened.

An attorney friend of mine who had worked in the federal system for many years said jurors walk into court assuming you are guilty, and the process the government is trained to follow is to destroy any credibility defendants have in the first few days. In doing so, when those defendants get up on the stand, the jury doesn't believe them, their witnesses, or their attorneys because they assume the "guilty party" must have also fooled those people too. This is why they go to great lengths to get people to plea, including using intimidation and threats—because they must win at any cost.

The Office of the Inspector General posted the following in the media for widespread distribution: "According to the indictment, the two men [Airport Director Ken Spirito and myself] *schemed* [italics mine] to obtain funding for PEX [People Express]. Spirito allegedly offered to help Morisi borrow $5 million from a local bank by guaranteeing the loan. The Peninsula Airport Authority agreed to grant the authority to cosign the loan to Spirito, who created three bank accounts. He then transferred misappropriated state and federal funds to the accounts and used the funds as collateral to guarantee the loan. Subsequently, PEX defaulted on the loan, and Spirito used the illicitly obtained funds to help Morisi make the payments."

Help Morisi make payments? To who? If it wasn't so disturbing how they manipulated the entire truth (let's face it, blatantly lied), it would have made me laugh. But this was no laughing matter. Remember, I could not respond to these news reports, even after they were picked up by the Associated Press and went national.

Spirito and I had *one meeting*. In that meeting, he suggested the idea of guaranteeing a loan for us, and that was my last communication with him or anything to do with the loan. Our CEO handled every subsequent meeting, signed all of the documents, and I barely even knew the terms until after they were signed. They used the bank the airport wanted under the terms they wanted, and it was all very secretive. Of course, all the attorneys involved, including ours—both in-house and outside corporate counsel—the bank's, and the airport's, agreed this was a legal use of airport funds. The government had to make this look like some well-planned scheme to use funds for a purpose other than what they were used for so anyone seated on a jury would arrive, biased and angry with us. Then they wouldn't—couldn't—listen to the truth.

And they were successful.

I could not believe Mr. Spirito was actually indicted on any charges related to the use of the funds. He relied on his counsel to advise him on the legality of this loan, and I heard he and all of the others agree that it was legal. I doubt the jury in his case heard a word from him or his defense team.

4

COUNSEL

Who is wise and understanding among you? Let them show it by their good life, by deeds done in the humility that comes from wisdom. But if you harbor bitter envy and selfish ambition in your hearts, do not boast about it or deny the truth. Such "wisdom" does not come down from heaven but is earthly, unspiritual, demonic. For where you have envy and selfish ambition, there you find disorder and every evil practice (James 3:13–14).

My trust in people had been decimated.

I consulted with a well-known local attorney, who was also the pastor of a large church, a man of God, who I believed I could trust. We had several meetings with his team, including another attorney who had clerked in a federal court for many years. Everyone agreed this was the biggest stretch of the "scheme statute" they had ever seen.

My attorney told me they could not charge me with the crimes they alleged, considering I was not an officer, had no corporate authority, and didn't sign on the bank account. For these reasons, he thought we could win the case in pre-trial motions and never have to go to trial. This was great news, and I felt immense relief. I believed God had matched me with this attorney for a purpose, one that would help me. In our last meeting together, my attorney told me he was calling the prosecutor that day and believed there was a possibility they would back off.

The next thing I heard from him was that he needed $150,000 to proceed. He gave no explanation. If the case was won in motions and didn't go to trial, I wondered, "Why so much?" He answered we would likely go to trial, and he had to be prepared for the costs involved with filing appeals.

What? Wow! My case had gone from "not prosecutable" to an "assurance of a guilty verdict requiring appeals." The government had control over every aspect, so they doubted a judge would let the prosecutors spend a bunch of money to bring this high-profile case to trial, just to lose in pre-trial motions, even if it made sense and was the "just" decision.

My attorney said there would be no way for me to be charged at the state level because only the feds have the right wording in their "scheme statute" to permit them to build a case around air. Remember, I was not an officer of the airline; I was not an authorized signer on the bank account, and I had no legal authority to spend the company money or make any decisions about spending alone. And the claims they had made about money being moved from the account were false—even easy to disprove! In other words, the crime never happened. The real question was, what was their motive here?

I found it difficult to believe this was all about adding a notch on the belt of a prosecutor desperate to become a judge, so much so that he had tossed any integrity or character aside. *Is this because the entire system is built on money, greed, and power?* I wondered.

I am hopeful someone will read my story, ask me questions about it, and do something to change the "justice" system. I believe there are thousands of others sitting in prison today for crimes they did not commit.

Back to my friend and attorney. Everything in his demeanor and his vigor for my case had changed after that one call to the prosecutor. To this day, I have no idea what was said on that call. Perhaps, the conversation turned personal, and an aggressive federal prosecutor, yearning to be appointed judge and build a high-profile case he did not intend to lose, who had already shown he could create a case out of nothing, weaponizing the IRS to look into anyone, caused my friend to have concerns about what they may try to do to him. I have no idea, but whatever was said, my attorney no longer wanted this case. He no longer wished to fight for me or for justice, nor had any interest in our friendship with me afterward. The news hit me like a cold shower, and I felt sad.

I contacted the public defender I had met at my initial hearing. She would schedule the hearing with the judge for us to get his approval for her to represent me. The date was set.

Imagine my surprise when a different attorney showed up and told me this was her case now. *What is happening?* I thought. This new attorney explained she handled these cases for this prosecutor. There was no further explanation, nor did she give me any opportunity to ask questions. This was when the full "scheme" became clear to me. I was up the injustice creek without an unbiased attorney paddle.

After the hearing, I shared with this public defender what my attorney had believed and told her I was certain God had a plan in this and trusted Him. Her response leveled my hope. "You better start trusting me because I am the only person who can keep you out of prison." *Prison?* I told her there was no way I could go to prison (in this country!) for crimes that never occurred. *"This is America!"* I told her. She chuckled as she shared why she became a public defender. The woman spoke about her years watching federal prosecutors deny people due process and a fair chance to defend themselves. She wanted to ensure everyone could get a good defense against these aggressive prosecutors determined to win at all costs. My stomach kissed my shoes as I realized there was a years' long history of manipulation in the judicial system, which she had seen with her own two eyes.

That evening, I told my wife about my serious concerns, about what the public defender had said, and how I didn't want her to represent me. "God must come first," she said. This attorney had actually told me *she* handled these cases *for this prosecutor,* and she and the prosecutor were "close friends." She reiterated it a few times, but upon seeing my face, followed it with, "It's not like we hang out around the BBQ at each other's houses, but we are close friends." She assured me her relationship with the prosecutor would not prevent her from fighting for me, which caused me to have more concerns, simply because she felt she needed to say that.

I explained to my wife that I had a much better feeling about the attorney initially assigned to me and wanted to get her back. So I left several messages for her, but she never responded. I considered going to the judge to get a different attorney; however, after inquiring the court clerk, I learned requesting a different attorney would not go well for me—that the judge would not grant it, and it would just upset the public defender I had.

The deck was set. The players were in place, right where the government wanted everyone.

5

MORE GAMES

---

*Above all else, guard your heart, for everything
you do flows from it* (Proverbs 4:23).

A few days later, I had my first in-person meeting with my public defender. Her smile intimated she was excited.

"I have great news that I've been waiting to tell you." She shared that she had met with the prosecutor, and he said he liked me, respected me, and appreciated my cooperation during the investigation, so he was going to make an offer. "I've never seen this from him before, especially this early." My heart rate ticked up as I thought, "Finally, they are dismissing everything!"

No. The deal was that he would dismiss sixteen of the eighteen charges if I plead guilty to two: one fraud charge and one tax evasion charge.

I didn't have to think, not for one second. "No, thank you."

This "deal" made it clear to me that the prosecutor knew he had no case and did not want to take a chance and go to trial. And I wasn't going to admit to something I didn't do.

This is where "the show" went to a whole new level. *My* attorney (emphasis on my) tried to convince me how lucky I was because in all the years she had worked with this guy, she had not seen him ever be so gracious. Her investigator echoed every word she said—I guess to add credibility to what she was saying.

Then she made the final push. "You have to decide quickly because he can withdraw the offer at any time."

Wow! This is a game! I thought. *And my attorney is on the opposite side!* She repeated the not-so-veiled threat multiple times to intimidate me.

"If you refuse, he will supersede indict you, with ten more charges that he'll find a way to add."

What? What about the truth?

I told her there was no way he could find anything to charge me with because there wasn't anything to start with. She chuckled. "Believe me, he will." She warned me he would spend the next six months leading up to the trial, searching to find someone—anyone—who would say I couldn't be trusted and put them on the stand during the trial.

"He can try. Let him go for it." She cautioned me again, saying he *would* find someone, likely several people. She even suggested they could use individuals I may not even know. There was no doubt these were tried-and-true tactics of which she was already well aware of. I realized that although she said she chose this career to help people, she had clearly become part of "the system" now and had forgotten why she became a public defender in the first place.

———

I read the original case from Waverly, Virginia, in which a guy was charged with running a drug empire.[2] During his trial, all four of the witnesses who testified against him were incarcerated at the time. The defendant claimed he had never met any of them, had evidence to prove the discrepancies in their stories, there were no drugs were found in his possession, no drug money had been located, and, to top it off, the local police chief testified there was no way he was a drug dealer. After several days of deliberation and some pressure from the judge to make a decision, the jury convicted him and sent him to prison.

After I read about this, concern and worry wrapped their tentacles around me. This was not justice. This was an abuse of power. And I was afraid I was quickly becoming the next victim.

The week after my initial in-person meeting, my public defender and I met again. She turned her computer screen toward me and showed me that because the airport director refused the plea offered to him and then spoke about his case to the media, the prosecutor had added twelve new charges in a superseded indictment. "See, I told you this is what happens, Mike. This is what he (the prosecutor) does." Then she said, "Mike, play the game, and you'll go home to your family."

Play the game . . .

This is no game! This is my life!

Over the next several days, weeks, and months, she said those words to my wife and me so many times that I hated hearing them. They made my insides swirl, threatening to erupt. This was certainly no game to us. She explained the prosecutor had exclusive selection of the jury and would seat one with no business owners so they would have no idea what operating a business or making tough decisions even looked like.

Is that even legal? I thought. *Don't both attorneys quiz the potential jury pool and give input?*

She wasn't finished with her not-so-veiled threats. "He will spend three days at trial, destroying your credibility so the jury won't even listen to me when our time comes to testify."

Then she laughed.

Continuing, my attorney admitted she used to sit in the courtroom just to watch him and the IRS criminal investigator destroy the credibility of defendants. She described it as a "work of art," to see them go after people and direct the path and outcomes of case after case. Listening to her disgusted me even more. *She is a fan of these guys!*

When I asked about the restitution they were demanding, nearly $500,000, she said she had mentioned it to him, but he needed the case to be above $250,000 in loss or it wouldn't be a felony, and the $500,000 made it a higher profile case. I was sure, somehow, he would imply to the jury I took that much for myself. There was no way I would burden my family with half a million in debt for money that was paid legally to tax liabilities, priority debts, and trust fund debts for a corporation I was not an officer of. But she made it clear: if we tried to change any of the terms from his initial offer, he would likely withdraw it and go to trial. Then I could lose my freedom and be incarcerated until trial and likely spend ten years in prison, away from my children, for a crime I didn't commit.

Oh, she was good. Grinch-good.

This restitution they demanded I repay included more than half of what was used to pay legal tax debt and trust fund debt for the company, and the rest was split between seven senior officers of the company: the CEO and counsel, who both remained on salary, and five of us who had worked over a year without pay. I was owed nearly $130,000 and received less than $66,000 total. My family is still burdened to this day with the repayment of money the company used to pay their legally owed debts. Figure out how that makes sense, and I will buy you dinner!

My attorney told me the prosecutor wanted to be a magistrate judge and needed this high-profile case. She even described how he should have been promoted after he handled a big pirate case years earlier. "They passed over him then so . . ." She sounded like a girl defending her boyfriend. I thought, *So I am supposed to admit to a crime that I not only did not commit, but that never even happened, to help him with his career? And this is the advice from my attorney?*

What a mess.

After a lot of thinking, praying, and soul-searching, I made a tough choice. With all of the threats and the obvious position my attorney was choosing, to not fight her "friend," the one who needed to win a high-profile case because she believed he deserved to be a judge, I went against everything I believed and accepted the plea deal.

I asked for a copy of the discovery she had received from the prosecution. Funny, my attorney had not even received it yet, and we had already plead the case—before she had any idea if he had any helpful evidence to present or not. When discovery finally came in, I wanted to see it all.

At first, my attorney stumbled through some excuse that the investigator was going through it. Then she offered me the opportunity to bring in an external hard drive so someone could download it for me. When I arrived a few days later with one I had purchased, she said she *just learned* she was not permitted to download anything to a hard drive I owned because she wasn't allowed to attach it to their computers. *You just learned this? After nine years in this role?*

Or maybe the prosecutor told her not to let me see it yet. Who knows?

"You know, I think I'm still allowed to go with another attorney who might take my case and go to trial. Just guessing."

At that point, she offered to download it, but only to a laptop if I brought one in.

It's OK to download it to my laptop but not a clean external hard drive? Everything turned ridiculous. Unfortunately, it was over one TB of information, so it wouldn't fit on a laptop.

She invited me to look through it at the office and copy anything I wanted, but when I arrived at our agreed upon time to do that, she suddenly realized she would have to sit a staff member with me to go through my discovery and didn't have the personnel resources to do that.

As I continued to push for the discovery, her investigator eventually sent me a signature card for an account held by the company at Bank of Hampton Roads. It had no signatures on it, but it had the names of the CEO and CFO and my name typed on it. Her assessment: "See, you were on the account." I was shocked to see my name on that document because there was never any intent for me to be on the account, and I had never signed to be on the account. I wasn't even employed by the airline when the account was opened. I sent the card to the bank and asked for all of the records for the account. I received a call two days later from a VP of the new bank (Bank of Hampton Roads had been acquired). He said he could not provide the records because I was not a signatory on the account and asked me where I got the signature card I sent them. When I told him from the federal prosecutor, he said it didn't come from the bank and refused to talk further about it under the advice of counsel.

What?

After that, I wanted all of the discovery, immediately! I thought, *Now, I can prove the prosecutor or someone in his office had fabricated evidence.*

I went back to my attorney's office, showed her the document she had sent me, and told her about the conversation with the banker. I was praising God because this was the chance I'd been waiting for to show this fiasco was a witch-hunt all along, and I had the proof the feds would go to any length to win their case, including fabricating documents, withholding exculpatory evidence, and lying to the grand jury by presenting contrived documents as "evidence." I told her this false "evidence" showed there was no case, and I wanted her to schedule a hearing in front of the judge, refuse the plea offer, and bring in the bank VP to testify. Excitement coursed through me. I knew

I had my chance to blow my case wide open and the prosecutorial corruption would be exposed.

What she said next startled me and made me sick. "Mike, you don't understand. This case is not about truth, not about guilt or innocence, and not about justice. He targeted you, and he will not lose. You could spend ten years in prison. Don't do this to your family. Just play the game, and you'll go home to your family."

I will never forget the cavalier way she said those words to me. So matter-of-fact. She admitted the system, and specifically this prosecutor within the system, would do anything to win at all costs because winning would get them rewarded. She admitted no one cares how they win, as long as they win.

My attorney laughed a little and said, "When this is over write a book; you'll make millions." I felt sick. It was the only good advice she gave me.

She finally sent a thumb drive to my wife in October 2020 with the discovery information, sixteen months after she had received it. Imagine that…she could download it to a thumb drive after all. When the discovery finally arrived and I went through it after I was released from prison, that signature card they showed me was not there. Dare I accuse a federal prosecutor of fabricating evidence and then hiding it? Not a chance. Dare I accuse my court-appointed public defender of sharing what I had learned about that document and said with the prosecutor? No way. It could have been omitted by mistake. Perhaps, it was just a coincidence. We may never know.

––––––––––

There needs to be sweeping re-education—and likely a reorganization—for these prosecutors on what their job actually is and a policy change on how they get recognition for a job well done. This business of being promoted when you win at all costs, including using illegal means like what I experienced, is beyond egregious.

One note I will add here: I believe public defenders in the federal system should not be employed by the government, working so closely with the prosecutors. They must be able to act on their own, regardless of how it affects the court proceedings or their peers across the aisle. For example, when I was adamant there was a falsified document in my discovery, I told my attorney this would blow the court wide open, that there could be dozens of appeals and motions coming before the court for every case this prosecutor had handled. He could have been punished or lost his job and license to practice law. Her response: "I would not let that happen, and the Court won't allow it. They will protect the integrity of the Court at all costs."

The only thing she left out was that we, the wrongly accused, the taxpayers, pay the price. The "integrity of the court?" The entire process, the judicial system, has little to no integrity from my perspective. I don't know if what she said is actual, written policy or if she was just trying to get me off the path of exposing the wrongdoing. Either way, it was wrong. If corruption exists, it must be brought to light.

6

SENTENCING

---

*Now faith is confidence in what we hope for and
assurance about what we do not see* (Hebrews 11:1).

Od is never wrong. Something God impressed upon me
when this part of my life first erupted proved to be true.
He whispered to my heart that many of my closest friends
would turn their backs on me. They would fall away, even talk
about me negatively—people I loved and who loved me. Close
friends. He also told me to let them go.

We never truly know what our friends think or say about
us when we aren't around, but God does. He also told me He
would send people I didn't expect who would end up walking
alongside me through this and helping my family, and I would
know He sent them. I eagerly awaited their arrival.

I can't tell you with mere words what it feels like to have people you have known and trusted for years simply turn their backs on you. And to have that choice be based on news reports. Some never even spoke to me about it. I realized through my crisis and the global pandemic that most people will accept whatever they hear on the news as truth and make life changes and decisions based on that information, without doing any research.

When did we become so gullible as a nation?

We've also learned friends will walk away from you if you disagree with them on social or political issues. And for many, once they have made up their minds about something, they do not want to hear the truth. Yes, God was right. It still hurt when it happened, but I found peace knowing if I let Him choose the people I let into my life, I'd be better off for it.

On the day I had to appear before the judge to have my plea accepted by the court, I felt sick. It wasn't the sniffles or a cough; I was sickened by what I was having to do. And every word spoken in that courtroom made me sicker.

When the judge asked me if I intentionally committed these crimes and if I was standing there having received no threats nor been intimidated, I paused as my eyes filled with tears. My attorney looked at me, and I noted the fear in her eyes. I assumed she was afraid of what I might say, then whispering at me to answer him. I told her I felt like I was going to throw up, that she knew I was lying under oath to a federal judge. She whispered again to play the game, and "You will go home to your family." The judge noticed our interaction because he asked me again if I was standing before him under no threat or intimidation, staring at me like he expected me to answer that I was not there voluntarily.

Looking back, I have often wondered if, at that moment, I had told him these crimes never happened, that I had proof someone submitted a fabricated signature card into evidence, and that the attorney standing next to me had threatened and intimidated me to take the plea or pay the price, what would have happened. But I had taken the bait of intimidation and was afraid they would, like she said, do everything in their power— which they have in spades—to ruin me and protect their own. Sentencing was set for October 2019.

———

As the date for sentencing neared, several meetings with my attorney brought some measure of peace that I would not be going to prison. In our last meeting, my wife and I felt confi- dent after she and her investigator, who had years of experience working with this judge, told us both, "No way [this judge] will send you to prison with your faith and the pastoral work you've done in this community over the past five years." Though she ended with the caveat that the final decision was up to the judge. This gave me some concern. But she seemed certain I would go home, reiterating her earlier assessment that being assigned to

Judge Allen was a blessing because she was a Christian who did not hide her faith, even to the point she had been cautioned about wearing a cross in court. Of course any judge has to handle each defendant equally and not consider their faith, but given the lack of intent and confusing circumstances around charging someone who was not an officer of a company, didn't sign on the account he was accused of moving funds out of, and his five years in local ministry, I felt like she may consider who I was in Christ as evidence that nothing was done to intentionally defraud anyone, nor was anyone defrauded from receiving money they were legally due. What I forgot was everything she knew about me was coming from the prosecutor, so little truth was ever shared with her.

The Bible says we can handle "all things through Christ who strengthens me" (Philippians 4:13), but this case would challenge me beyond what I believed I could handle. But isn't that how He does it, when He has a big plan and chooses someone to fulfill it? Often, God creates or allows something so big, we *can't* handle it on our own and recognize how much we need Him. It's our faith in the midst of struggles that He seeks.

The sentencing date was pushed out to February 20, 2020 because of the prosecutor's heavy case schedule, which was good because I knew without a doubt I would be with my family for Christmas.

Sentencing day finally arrived, and my wife and I, and so many good friends who joined us, expected God to intervene as only He can to put a stop to all this mess. Maybe He wouldn't orchestrate some crazy revelation by the judge, like exposing that I had been targeted and charged with moving money that was never even moved, but I hoped I would at least be permitted to head home to serve my sentence while still living with my family and working to provide financial support.

When we arrived, the first order of business was to get approval for self-surrender in the event I was sentenced to incarceration, which the judge agreed to with no objection from the prosecutor. I felt good about that, again believing there would be no prison sentence. The prosecutor began by speaking highly about my service to the homeless of Norfolk, feeding those who were hungry, holding church services in the streets of downtown, and more. He spoke of the surprising number and endearing content of the letters, character references, they had received.

"Some of the best I've ever read," he said.

I felt good, but then my world came crashing down. Immediately after the praise, he showed his true colors and launched into a long, descriptive account of the crimes he was accusing me of, with a vengeance that made me want to jump up and call him a liar in open court. As he spoke about the money "moved out of an account to avoid payment of a lien," (I wondered why a judge wouldn't stop him right there for clarification, knowing there is no way can money can be moved from an account after a lien is in place), how I placed funds I withdrew in a new account at another bank, and how I then closed the account so creditors couldn't find us, I was outraged.

I turned to my attorney and asked her to ask the prosecutor for the bank records that showed these funds being moved. I asked her to tell the judge that none of the things he was accusing me of ever happened, and we could prove it in five minutes. Every statement he made about my actions was a lie.

The prosecutor repeated that although the many letters of reference they received were some of the best he had ever read and portrayed me as the man he had come to know, he felt they proved I wasn't remorseful because no one mentioned anything in their letters about me being so. Then, to sucker-punch me further, he said, "Given Mr. Morisi's high profile in the community, it is especially important that his sentence serve as a deterrent to others" (my paraphrase), and he recommended I go to prison for twenty-seven months, the minimum based on the guidelines.

Eventually, my attorney got her chance to fight back. Sitting there, listening to him, she acknowledged she knew everything he was saying about my handling of that account was false and never happened. But she also made it clear she could not challenge anything he said because we had a plea agreement. *Could* not or *would* not? Help me understand why a plea agreement gives the prosecutor license to lie and straps the defense attorney from telling the judge he was doing so? It made me wonder what kind of justice system we have in America.

I told her when it came time for me to speak, I fully intended to tell the judge the three things he accused me of were lies and could easily validate them as such. She told me that if I said anything, the judge would cancel my self-surrender and send me to prison right then, and I'd probably serve at least five years. I could not believe what I was hearing. I hope no one reading this is willing to tolerate such a miscarriage of justice, which I fear takes place often in our federal system.

That I had to listen to a prosecutor lie about what I had done, knowing if I pointed it out, I would get punished, infuriated me. My attorney stood up and spoke for a few minutes about my five years of service to the community—feeding and serving the poor and homeless—mentioned my close family dynamics, including that I had young children, and then sat down. I had several friends in court, and they were all shocked, each one saying afterward they felt like they could have done a better job representing me.

I believe my attorney and the prosecutor had already planned out how that morning would go. She had told me that my friends would have a chance to speak, but once we were seated in court, she told me the prosecutor wouldn't allow it. I don't know if that was true or even if prosecutors have any authority to stop that step, but she was focused on the agenda she had all along—to protect him at all costs, even at the cost of trashing her own character.

I did my best to show remorse and stayed calm as I shared with the judge for my permitted two minutes. But it was too late. The judge had watched my reactions to what had been said in the courtroom up to that point and erroneously determined my behavior was proof of my lack of remorse. When I was finished, the judge went on and on about the perceived lack of remorse and how, as a man of faith, I should've stopped the misuse of funds. It was apparent to me; she had decided, maybe even before we walked into the courtroom.

This left me with no choice but to also question the highest role in the court system. Some judges, I believe, have forgotten the individuals in front of them are real people, deeply affected by their decisions, and the lives of families are forever impacted by the rulings they make. Maybe they are tired, perhaps jaded by what they encounter every day, or maybe they are oblivious to what some prosecutors are doing. Maybe they are in their roles without the requisite experience to be and got appointed because of political affiliations. I don't have the answers, but these questions should be explored.

At some point, they have a responsibility to question some of the thing's prosecutors say, and if they truly listened to people—all people—they would hear the inconsistencies, the things that just don't add up. Are they listening? I believe many, have become part of a machine that cranks things out without considering the people involved or, perhaps, they don't care. Remember my statistic from the introduction? The United States has less than 5 percent of the world's population; yet we have almost 25 percent of the world's total prison population. Someone needs to care about that and start looking into how that is happening.

The judge sentenced me to twenty-four months in prison, and I had to report in thirty days. There seemed to be no regard that this so-called offense was alleged to have happened six years before nor for the work I had done since then. My entire world crashed in on me at that moment. I can't remember a time in my life where I was so mad.

I admit, in that courtroom, I felt like God had abandoned me. How could He possibly think I could handle being away from my wife and children for two years for something I did not do? I didn't even know how to pray, but my wife was so calm about it—so confident in God's promises. Her first words were, "The Lord spoke to me and told me to read Isaiah 55:8–9." The verses say, "'For my thoughts are not your thoughts, neither are your ways my ways,' declares the Lord. 'As the heavens are higher than the earth, so are my ways higher than your ways and my thoughts than your thoughts.'" This brought her such peace because it revealed to her He was still in control. That He was doing this for a reason, and His plans are always good. I admired her peace and trust but wasn't feeling it for myself right then. All I could think about was my life without my wife and kids, how my boys would feel about their dad being in prison, even about what their friends would say. How would my wife afford to live without my income? All of that rushed through my head, along with how angry I was at the miscarriage of justice and poor, unprofessional handling of my case by my appointed counsel. I confronted my attorney in the hallway, but she was only worried the judge would hear me and send me to prison. I believe she was more concerned about what I was saying than about her handling of the case.

The prosecutor told the judge he would file a Rule 35 for a 50 percent reduction of sentence if I met with them about the case involving the airport director, whose trial would start in two weeks. I agreed but knew I didn't have anything to offer.

Still raw from the sentencing, a couple of days later, I went to meet with the prosecutor's team. He had assembled a large group to hear what I knew about the case against the airport director. It was quite a disappointment for me to see the inner workings of how a trial is planned. During the hour-long discussion primarily about the loan, I made it clear, based on what little I knew about the loan, the airport director should not be the one they charged because so many—including much more powerful people like the attorneys who had approved it—were involved in making it happen. "These power brokers in Newport News picked the bank we would use, the terms of the loan, and how it would be processed and distributed," I explained.

That wasn't what the team wanted to hear. I mentioned that I had personally heard the airport attorney approve the use of funds. That attorney assured all of us it was legal. They argued, "The attorney said the airport could use the funds to guarantee the loan but never said they could actually use the funds to pay it off if you defaulted." Maybe you're thinking what I was: *that's ridiculous. It's just a word game.* Just when I thought I had seen and heard it all, I realized they had worked out something to keep the attorney from bearing any responsibility for his guidance.

The airport director and I had started out as friends, but we had a falling out and had not spoken in several years. We were not friendly with each other anymore and had even engaged in some heated exchanges over the company's refusal to use his marketing director for our advertising efforts. But all I had to say to the prosecutor's team was that I knew he should not be charged for anything pertaining to this loan agreement. How he handled setting it up and reporting it was another story, but I knew nothing about that.

The next exchange between the team and me injected fresh anger into my soul. They told me to return a few days later for two to three hours of "witness prep." I laughed because I had heard this type of pre-trial "preparation" went on, but I could not believe it was actually happening. The interesting thing was, when I told them I didn't need to be prepped because I was just going to tell the truth, they decided not to put me on the stand. What I knew to be true about the airport director's actions regarding the loan and the assurances from several attorneys that it was a legal and an appropriate use of funds did not align with the case they planned to present.

Thankfully, I was not required to testify to get the deal. The prosecutor told me he would file the Rule 35 and my counsel confirmed, "You will get a 50 percent reduction in your sentence." Though . . . it was all dependent on the prosecutor following through with what he had promised.

Nearly eight months later, after dozens of letters and excuses, I finally got an eight-month reduction (not the full 50 percent per the deal), but it was hard not to think of that eight months as a blessing after all I had seen and experienced, so I was grateful for that.

7
DELAYS

For we do not wrestle against flesh and blood, but
against the rulers, against the authorities, against the
cosmic powers over this present darkness, against
the spiritual forces of evil in the heavenly places
(Ephesians 6:12).

I was to report to the Petersburg Minimum Security Camp on
March 20, just thirty days later. I knew much preparation was
needed, but I could not wrap my head around this. We often
say God only gives us what He knows we can handle. He must
believe I am really strong. I'm not sure. But I remained stead-
fast in my belief that God will put us in situations to see if we
will surrender to His strength to get through it.

When I lost my son when he was twenty-five, back in 2012,
I fell apart, and my behavior reflected the truth that I didn't have

it all together. Then one day, God woke me up and showed me my son was with Him. In that revelation, I found a peace I never imagined I could feel in that loss. I know I will see my son again—get to hug him and talk with him and walk in Heaven with him. I found peace in the midst of my heartache over losing him. I found a deep knowing, that God would always be there to comfort us regardless of what seems like unbearable pain. Yet, there I was, questioning God's faithfulness in this trial (i.e., in my suffering, not the courtroom trial anymore).

People ask me all the time why God would let me go through what I did, why He would allow this to happen to me, why He'd allow these individuals to railroad me as they did. I don't believe He did just *allow it*. If you read the Bible, you might get a different perspective. A very dear friend reminded me; In Psalm 105:16–19, it says, "God called down famine on the land and destroyed all of their supplies of food; and *he sent a man before them*—Joseph sold as a slave. They bruised his feet with shackles, his neck was put in irons, till what he foretold came to pass, till the word of the Lord proved him true" (italics mine). The Lord chose Joseph and sent him into slavery, into prison, knowing all along, he would rise in strength and maturity and become the leader who would bring the people out of the famine. God had a plan, chose His warrior, and sent him.

I see now what God did as far as my story goes, but it took me a while to get to this point. I had to struggle with it before getting this revelation that He had a plan when He sent me.

During my thirty days of waiting to self-surrender, preparing my family to be without me, preparing my heart—which was shattered and likely going to be broken even more—the

COVID-19 pandemic began. I received a call from my former public defender. She had filed a motion to delay my surrender until April 30 (everyone believing the shutdown would be over by then). This was good news, and now I was really celebrating the Lord. I had accepted that I was going away and had confidence He would protect me and care for my family while I was away. My prayers stopped being "Lord, don't send me" and turned into "Lord, I love you; I don't want to go but believe in Your promises and praise You with all my heart."

I still wondered, though, was He going to take "this cup from me" (Matthew 26:39) because I was faithful and praising Him as planned for prison? Was I going to be allowed to stay home? The public defender filed the motion, and the judge extended my report date to April 29, 2020.

In late March, Attorney General Barr announced that the Bureau of Prisons and Courts were to use home confinement for any non-violent defendants sentenced to twenty-four months or less and not transfer anyone to federal prisons because of the risk from the pandemic. News reports indicated that current inmates at Petersburg were being released so of course they won't send me there.

This is it!

Our prayers had been answered. We felt excitement about this and praised God that I could stay home.

My public defender contacted me shortly after this announcement and let me know she was filing a motion to modify my sentence to home confinement. The airport director had been sentenced to home confinement for his conviction on twenty-two felonies. Several inmates from Petersburg, some with over twenty-four months remaining on their sentences were coming home, so we thought this was a done deal. God had removed the thorn (2 Corinthians 12:7). The next day, she *wrote* to tell me the judge extended my self-surrender to July 29, explaining she did not ask for the modification of the sentence to home confinement because the prosecutor told her he would object. Here is the transcript from the email after I sent her the statement from Attorney General Barr regarding the order to modify sentences and not send anyone to federal prisons because of the covid outbreak:

On March 30, 2020, at 16:09, "Federal Public Defender" wrote:

Hello: Please be advised that I am in receipt of your previous emails. Please note that the Defender Community is providing almost hourly updates on the COVID-19 pandemic, and my colleagues and I are receiving over 100 emails a day, many of which are updates regarding COVID-19 and our incarcerated clients. While I understand that your emails are meant to provide information about COVID-19, I more than likely already have that information and I am receiving more up-to-date information that the public is being given.

I have drafted a motion seeking two different types of relief in your case in light of COVID-19. The first is to seek an additional extension of the April 30, 2020, self-surrender date and the other one is seeking to con-

vert your sentence of incarceration to home confinement with electronic monitoring.

Accordingly, I have reached out to AUSA for his position on my proposed Motion and they are not opposed to a 60 day extension of your self-surrender, but they do oppose your sentence being converted to home confinement with electronic monitoring.

I sent an email in response, seeing if they would agree to an extension of 90 days, as opposed to 60 days, and he is agreeable to a 90 day extension.

At this point, since AUSA is not opposed to extending the self-surrender date for 90 days, I am going to file the Motion to Extend the Self-Surrender date as this is the best possible avenue to have you remain out-of-custody, awaiting your self-surrender date.

Once we get closer to the new date, provided that Judge Allen grants my Second Unopposed Motion to Extend the Self-Surrender Date, we will reevaluate the COVID-19 situation and then determine what motions, if any, will be ethically and necessary to file. I will file the Second Motion to Extend tomorrow.

Thanks, KRK Assistant Federal Public Defender

In a follow up phone conversation, she tried to convince me that for her to file for the home confinement, knowing about the prosecutor's objection, would be considered frivolous by the Court. I am not an attorney but believe most defense attorneys would follow through with what they knew to be best for their client, and in compliance with the AG Order, regardless of how the prosecutor felt or what they wanted. And the Court should expect prosecutors to object and defense attorneys to fight and consider everything presented while making a fair ruling. Isn't that what defense attorneys do, fight for their clients? I considered this a simple and relevant request since the attorney general of the United States had issued an order in a global pandemic. So regardless of what the prosecutor "thought," I believe the judge would have granted the motion to comply with the AG order. You see she even went so far as to imply pushing this could get me incarcerated in jail now awaiting transfer to the federal facility. She was so good at manipulation.

The representation I had was still (and always had been) focused more on what the prosecutor wanted than what was right, just, or in the best interest for me.

In her next email, later that same day, she was upset, learning for the first time that I had written a personal letter to the judge back in February, asking her for consideration to modify my sentence. I had received a letter from my public defender that her services had been completed, so I sent the letter *pro se*, or self-represented. I assumed I could and wanted to do everything I could to protect my family. What I learned after sending it was that letters written directly to the judge are generally left unread. In the next email, the public defender I was again forced to count on to represent me wrote this after learning about the letter I had sent months earlier:

As hard as Susan and I have worked on your case and on your behalf, notice about the letter that you sent to Judge Allen would have been appropriate and welcomed.

AUSA has reached out to me about the letter, which was just filed electronically, and while yesterday he was agreeable to the 90 day extension of your self-surrender date, and I filed my pleading this morning indicating as such, I do not know now, in light of your letter, whether he will change his mind and object to an additional extension on your self-surrender.

I plan to call him as soon as I have the opportunity to discuss this issue, and I will keep you apprised of the update. I hope that you understand the gravity of your actions and that you understand further that you have seriously jeopardized your case and your freedom by filing this letter without my knowledge.

KRK, Assistant Federal Public Defender

So clearly, not only did the prosecutor object to compliance with the attorney general's order regarding non-violent convictions and prison time for twenty-four months or less, but now, because I had written the judge, asking for mercy once I was no longer represented by counsel, they were threatening me with my freedom—not for a legal violation but, presumably, because my actions threatened their plan.

These puppets of the system control every step of the process because if one step is missed or plays outside their scheme, they may lose what they are seeking . . . a win. Research shows that 97 percent of federal cases are plead out and 96 percent are won.[3] My particular prosecutor has even higher stats.[4] To me, those stats are red flags. They do not mean investigators and prosecutors are doing a great job of putting away criminals; they mean they are structuring cases to win, regardless of guilt. And if you don't agree to their plea offers, they make it clear, they will increase the number of charges filed and you will spend a very long time in prison, even for crimes you didn't commit.

In subsequent emails, my counsel refused to work on my behalf for any change or modification to the sentence or for my time between March 20 and July 29 to be served in home confinement and counted toward my sentence. She was so angry with me that every communication moving forward included language stating she no longer wanted to help me. And she said, the Rule 35 agreement we had, which was communicated to the judge, was no longer available. Her email:

You are incredibly lucky that my Motion to Extend the Self-Surrender Date was granted before AUSA had an opportunity to withdraw his agreement to the 90 day extension.

Do not ask if this time can be considered as home confinement. I will not file a motion requesting that it be considered home confinement.

Based upon your letter, the possibility of a Rule 35 sentence reduction is nonexistent.

KRK, Assistant Federal Public Defender

Anger swirled inside me, too, because of the injustices and obvious failures of my counsel to properly represent me, but oddly, I also felt peace. I knew now God was in control, and although I did not want what was ahead, I made it clear to Him, I wanted it to be His will, not mine. That is not an easy prayer.

Through faith, I continued to believe I would not have to go to prison. COVID-19 was rampant through the federal prison system, and inmates and guards were dying. The prison system could not handle the virus's storm through our society. That said, I had told God long ago to "send me" wherever He needed me.

My family now had four months to prepare—financially and emotionally—so I got to work.

My twelve-year-old woke up one morning and told me God had spoken to him, telling him I was going on a "mission trip for Him." What he shared was a vivid recollection, a clear message he believed was from the Lord.

My older son likened it to his many friends whose dads were deployed in the military; he would look at my leaving as a deployment.

They seemed to be handling this much better than me.

My wife was as amazing as always; she trusted the Lord and knew no matter what, He would take care of all of us. She believed His plan, whatever it was, was for His glory and the best for us in the long run. My entire family was giving me peace.

At the time of all this, I was not only in ministry; I was selling real estate, and what God did to bring clients to me rocked me with humility. He was at work for me to secure my family financially. I had two new clients who told me they prayed for God to send them an honest real estate agent, and only God could send them a convicted felon getting ready to report to prison in answer to their prayer. Isn't that funny to think!

I still held out some hope the path would change but really wanted to honor Him as my Father and trust in Him, even if it didn't make sense to me. And His plan would soon become clear.

Typically, for a twenty-four-month sentence, after "good time credit," people served about twenty months, then had probation for three years. That was what we all expected to happen to me. However, deep down, for some reason I couldn't explain, I felt like I would only be there for two or three months, despite how the prosecutor was determined to keep me there. After all, I had dared to write a letter to the judge asking for her grace!

July 29 arrived.

This is where writing my story gets tough. I went from angry at a broken, disturbing system of justice, one filled with power, greed, deception, and manipulation, to enduring a prison system that has one mission: to break you. The one thing that gave me peace as I continued my journey was my heart believed God is sovereign, and I knew He never owes me an explanation for the things He does. He could have stopped this journey at any step of the way, but He didn't, and when I prayed and told Him "by Your will Lord, not mine," as scary as that sounds, it was (and is) how I felt.

That morning that I reported to the authorities, my eyes filled with tears, my arms gave hugs, and my lips offered prayers and promises of trusting the Lord with what our family would go through next. The one-hour drive was quiet, and the realization of what we knew was coming settled like dust during a demolition and became our reality. To kiss my wife and boys goodbye for up to twenty months was one of the hardest things I've had to do. We are a very close family. Always lots of hugs and snuggles, ongoing prayer, seeking the Lord, reading the Bible and studying devotionals together, and watching movies together every Friday night. I was going to miss the rides to school, the sporting events, everything. More than anything, we love being together and always made time for laughter and together time despite our busy lives.

This hurt a lot.

8

SURRENDER

*Bring to an end the violence of the wicked and make
the righteous secure—you, the righteous God who
probes minds and hearts* (Psalm 7:9).

As I said goodbye, I told my family I would talk to them later that evening. I said that with confidence because I had called the prison the day before to discuss what I could bring, what to expect, and if I would have access to a phone that first day. They assured me I would.

The first person to meet me was a prison captain, who asked me if I knew anyone currently incarcerated in the camp. "No. Any I did know were sent home early because of the pandemic."

He asked me if I had any concerns about being mixed in the camp with other prisoners. I said no. Then he told me there were drugs, cell phones, and alcohol in the camp, and if I messed with any of it and got caught, he would transfer me far away from my family. I assured him I would not be involved in any of that. After all, I was a pastor, right? I had been living to please God for many years, I told him, so he did not have to be concerned about me.

"I've heard that before."

Getting registered was smooth and easy and included interviews with a psychologist, a nurse, someone who took more fingerprints and pictures, and others. They dressed me in a size XXXL pair of underwear, 4X t-shirt, and 6X orange jumpsuit for the initial twenty-one days of quarantine, which I had to be in to make sure I didn't have covid. I thought it was a joke because I wear size large in everything. It was the first step toward their taking control over me and the first time I realized they couldn't care less about my comfort. I saw shelves full of size large in everything, but the officer gave me what he did and didn't appreciate me questioning him. There was no doubt . . . *I am in prison now.*

They handed me a packet and told me it contained envelopes and stamps and paper. That was a lie. There were envelopes but no stamps or paper.

I got to my cell at 2:30 p.m., and when the gate closed, an eerie feeling came over me. My cell was one in a row of about six cells, but at least there was air conditioning because the block was used only for covid quarantine. Scanning my surroundings, I noted one television hung in the middle of the row, which essentially meant only the tenant of one cell could see it. I was already missing my family. Before leaving, I asked the officer what time I could use the phone, but he ignored me and walked away. Then he stopped and yelled back, "Don't drink the water in that sink!"

I later learned the building had been condemned several years before, but when the pandemic hit, it was painted to look functional, air conditioning units were installed, and was put back in service. The moldy smell, a musty odor, not unlike the smell of sweaty socks, was strong, and a glance at the walls revealed black mold right under the fresh coat of paint. My heart dropped. A building deemed illegal to house anyone from off the street was declared suitable to house inmates in quarantine. *Here we go*, I thought, *life in our government's prison system.*

When I saw him again, I asked the officer for water or food and was quickly told lunch/dinner *(linner?)* had been served at noon; there would be no food or water until breakfast at 6:00 a.m. "I have to go fifteen hours with no water (since I was told not to drink from the sink) and no food?"

His reply: "Yep!"

"What about the phone?"

He laughed alongside the prison counselor assigned to the block, who was standing there too. I later learned prison counselors are not trained in mental health assessment or treatment; they are simply given that title. "You won't get the phone until quarantine is over."

"That's twenty-one days!" There was no way could I go three weeks without talking to my family. "There must be a mistake. I was told both on the phone before reporting and by the guy when I checked in that I could use the phone today."

He laughed again. "Welcome to prison. They lied to you. It's called 'spinning you.' They don't want to deal with your question, so they answer in a way that will please you so you stop asking."

Once again, I couldn't contain the thought that God had turned His back on me. I allowed the enemy to get into my head and felt so lost, angry, frustrated . . . and alone. The feeling of the total loss of control over your life is not something you can understand unless you've experienced it. And when you lose that control and become dependent on people who don't care about you, whether you live, or how uncomfortable you are, who will lie to your face and even do things intentionally to make your life worse . . . well, it causes a deep sense of grief, despair, and hopelessness. Those are all tools in the enemy's bag of destruction, which he uses to make us believe God has left us.

That I may not speak to my wife for twenty-one days brought an even deeper sense of dread. I can't adequately describe it. I had figured that no matter how bad things got, if I could at least talk to my best friend, I believed I would be OK. I had a hard time thinking God knew what He was doing and even doubted His plans were always best. To this day, I wonder about this first day in prison and His part in it, but then I rest easy, knowing He walked through it with me. Looking back, I realized what He wanted for me in all the chaos: zero distractions. He just wanted me to be with Him.

———

At 4 p.m. on that first day, a new officer arrived, and we spoke for a half hour. He was kind and thoughtful and ended up getting me some food and several bottles of water. He also told me I could ask the counselor in the morning if she would get me access to the phone assuring me I would not have to go 21 days without it and even apologized for the behavior of the other officers. He admitted it was embarrassing to see how they treated us. I asked him for a Bible; he agreed to look for one.

The inmate in the cell next to me told me he was leaving in the morning and would leave me his Bible. I sat on my bed and endured the longest night of my life. The thoughts that go through your mind if you let the enemy talk to you are crazy but so easy to succumb to. It took me about four hours to figure out how I could wrap a sheet around my neck, tie it to the fixed bars and the gate, and when they saw me "hanging there," they would hit the button to open the gate and that action would break my neck. The idea of taking my life never entered my mind, but the realization of how easy it would be to do it did. I had always believed God's Word to be true, but I was convinced He had turned His back on me. And I let Him know what I thought about that. When God created me, He designed me with a minimal filter, so when I get upset, it's obvious. I am sure He was not surprised by my questions and the anger and disappointment I expressed to Him. I don't know what time I finally fell asleep, but when I did, for the first time since I came to know Jesus, I felt alone—truly alone.

I may have slept only a couple of hours when the lights punched on and officers strode down the hallway, conducting their shift change count. I was told when I checked in that we had to stand for the count. I later learned that did not apply in this block of cells. Nonetheless, I jumped up, clad in only my way-too-big boxers, and noticed one of the officers was a female. Immediately, I apologized for not being dressed. She seemed to take offense at my apology, making it clear she did not care how I was dressed and had no interest in seeing anything I had.

I had not only lost my freedom, but I was at the mercy of people who hated their jobs and the people they were charged to supervise.

Not even twenty-four hours in, I heard countless guys yelling and cussing at officers, and I thought, "It's no wonder. The treatment is demeaning, and no one respects anyone." One inmate in a cell a few away from mine yelled at me, warning me to stop being so nice. "They just abuse guys like you," he said. "You have to cuss them out and threaten that your wife will call the media; then they will do something for you."

As he'd promised, the inmate in the cell next to me put his Bible and shower shoes through the food slot into my cell before he left at 5:00 a.m. Interestingly, I learned that in prison, you can count on what inmates say they will do, but rarely ever can you believe what you hear from the guards and other staff. I grabbed the Bible from the shelf where food gets pushed through and opened it, soaking in God's Word like salve on a wound.

At 6:30, the staff brought "breakfast," which was packaged sugary stuff, muffins and pastries expired for months, two small cartons of milk, and a piece of fruit—that day an apple. Some days, a banana. All I ate was the banana. I drank both cartons of milk; it was the first time I'd had milk in years.

Later, I met an inmate trustee—prisoners who had access to everything with little to no supervision—who noticed my Bible on my bed, and he asked me if I was a believer. He would become a good friend during my time in that cell, and he always brought me extra fruit and lots of bottles of water, paper, envelopes, and other "goodies."

The crazy thing is, you learn quickly that if you get extra bottles of water, you better hide them because the guards will take them from you, even though they know we can't drink the water from the sink. You are allocated two bottles per day. That's it. The trustee and I prayed together, and he seemed happy despite his more than ten years being locked up, with fourteen more ahead. He just woke up every day and asked the Lord to watch out for him and show him how to bring Him glory while he was there. This man became such a blessing—surely one of the people God put in my path to support my faith.

I had a Bible, which I read daily for eight to ten hours, and another Christian to talk to. For three days, I asked the guards about using the phone, and each time, I was brushed off. About that third day, the counselor finally came through and confirmed there was no way for me to get access to the phone because I had to register on their computer, and they didn't allow inmates to do that until the quarantine period was over. I broke down in tears. In eighteen years, I had not gone a day without talking to my wife.

This propelled me into feeling upset with God all over again. How could He let this happen to our family? I knew my wife must have been going crazy with worry. I was going crazy with worry. No television, no radio, no newspapers, no information, and no idea how my family was handling this. The counselor agreed to call my wife and let her know I could not call until I got to the camp.

Afterward, she came back to tell me how nice my wife was. This would become important later.

———————

How many of us realize faith is more than just how we behave and about following the Ten Commandments? It is about heart transformation, not behavior modification. Once we get the revelation of who God is and who we are, we are obedient, out of our love for Him. In this case, the point is, besides what's listed in the Ten Commandments, worry, anxiety, unforgiveness, bitterness, shame, and condemnation are all sins because they come from a place of not trusting in the sovereignty and faithfulness of God. We focus on our circumstances rather than on Jesus. It would take me several weeks inside prison to remember this. The good news is that God does not give up on us.

It was unnerving to live in the prison environment. Officers tasked with conducting hourly rounds to check on the welfare of inmates, those of us who had no way of communicating with them, regularly skipped the rounds, sometimes for many hours. During my first few days there, the guards disappeared for three or four hours every afternoon. Other inmates talked about it and hoped if anything went wrong, they could make enough noise to get their attention.

It was cool how I got to know the inmates on the block having never seen them. They would yell over to me and assure me they would help if I needed anything; they passed food items back and forth if a guy was extra hungry. Once every three days, we could get out to walk to the end of the block where the showers were, one at a time, but I actually met the other guys on that walk. The guards simply opened a cell and let us go, sometimes not coming back for an hour or so, giving us time for conversation. Of course, another thing that was missing was privacy. The shower stall was private from the other inmates, but if guards walked in, male or female, they could see you in the shower. Some female guards would actually stop and talk to you while you were showering, which was not comfortable for me at all! Most were respectful, but there were always one or two who cared little (if at all) how their actions made you feel.

On my fourth day, I spoke with an evening-shift lieutenant about the phone privilege, and she assured me what I had been told was not true. The counselor was supposed to give me access to a phone, and she would leave that message in the morning. Elation coursed through me. Could this be a breakthrough?

No. That was the last I heard from that guard, and the counselor insisted there was no way to make it happen. Then she moved me into another cell block. There were seven cells lined in a row, but they were all empty. She let me choose the one I wanted, so when I spied a single television in the middle of the hall, something I had not seen in five days, I chose the one right in front of it. I asked her to put it on TBN (Trinity Broadcasting Network). She had no idea what TBN was, but we found it.

As she walked away, I said half-jokingly, don't let them forget about me back here. It was 9:30 a.m. I next saw someone around noon when trustees found me for lunch. No officer came in until around 3:30 in the afternoon, when the shift change count happened, and they admitted they did not know I was back there. They couldn't find me, and that's when a trustee told them where I was.

The evening shift officer was the one I mentioned earlier, the good man, and we ended up talking that night for nearly two hours as he stood outside my cell. I had been watching TBN all day, so I felt closer to the Lord than I had since arriving. He left to handle some business and came back around 11 p.m. with the overnight officer. She was not nearly as friendly. I understand they aren't there to be friendly.

I never saw her again—or anyone else until 7:00 a.m. when medical arrived for my daily temperature check. I had missed breakfast, and the guards told me there was nothing they could do about it. Thankfully, the trustee buddy came back around nine and loaded me up because he was going to be off for the next two days. He gave me so many bottles of water and snacks and bananas that I had to hide everything under my 6X jumpsuit, which was on top of my bunk, or the other guards would take it all. I know this sounds ridiculous, but it's daily life in the Bureau of Prisons.

I figured out other tricks too. I used the huge jumpsuit to dry off with after showers and between shower days, and I used it as a sheet to hang in my cell for some privacy as I stood naked at the sink to freshen up and handwash my underwear. Then I'd wrap the sheet around me until my underwear dried while hanging on my bed. Every day, guards promised me towels and more clothes, but it wasn't until day thirteen I finally had a towel and some extra underwear.

I left the TV on all night on TBN and heard many powerful and uplifting messages. I just knew the Lord had planned this for me. With each story or show, I experienced moments when I felt strongly that God was saying, "That word was for you." It gave me confidence. He was truly with me, and if I would just relax, He would take care of everything.

My primary issue continued to be no contact with my family. On the morning of day eight, everything changed for me. I woke up to the presence of Jesus sitting on my bed.

Look, I know some of you may want to put the book down now, but stick with me, please. As I tell you about how He showed up and what happened over the next six days, I hope you will begin to understand who He is in your life, too. I hope you'll get to know Him as intimately as I did, once you fully surrender to Him . . . as I did.

Each morning for those next six days, I woke up and said good morning to Jesus. Then I read the Bible out loud. As I read, I stopped periodically and asked Him questions. And I got answers. I didn't hear the audible voice of Jesus, but more of an internal voice, centered in my heart. Believe me, He is always speaking to us. We just have to want to listen.

At times, I heard Him tell me to put the Bible down and watch a message coming up on TBN. By now, the block was full of other inmates, and they all came in complaining about having to listen to "this Christian stuff." They were usually pretty vocal about it too. But I asked the officers to leave it on, and they did. Sometimes, the officers would even stop and hang out, listening to whatever program was airing.

After about three or four days, one new officer came in and changed the channel because he didn't "want to hear that" every time he walked through. Sadness creeped in, but in the next instant, the entire block of guys yelled at him to put it back on. And I mean everyone. The seeds of hope and truth that TBN had unknowingly planted in them were beginning to bear fruit, and I was thrilled. We all agreed the officers could change the TV station at 4:00 for the local and national news, then turn it back to TBN at 7:00, so that's what we did.

On shower days, the guys started calling me "Pastor" and stopped me as I walked past their cells to ask me questions about God. The guys on either side of me on the block spoke to me about Jesus, and I would pray for them. I noticed their change. Several asked for Bibles. It was a beautiful thing to witness. Jesus, whose presence was still showing up in the morning, beamed as more of His sons experienced heart transformation. I felt humbled to be there, to share His love with these guys, most of whom had been in prison for a long time. The man in the cell next to me came in at age nineteen and had served twenty years of a forty-three-year sentence. He had committed some terrible crimes. His story was a sad one, but I believe today, he is still following Jesus, and I wish I could see the impact he is having on the guys he is housed with now. One day it will be revealed to me.

Around the eleventh day in my new cell, I again asked the counselor to help me get time on the phone. My soul ached after not talking to my wife or hearing her voice or those of my children for nearly two weeks. Again, the counselor told me I couldn't because to do so, I would have to get on the computer to reserve it, and that wasn't permitted during covid. The inmate in the cell next to me yelled out, "She is a liar!" He said the "phone people" bring a piece of paper and you just fill it out. Then they get you a code for the phone in a few hours. The counselor looked stunned. I asked her, with in tears filling my eyes, "Have you been lying to me all along?"

She uttered some expletives and walked away, obviously embarrassed. After that, she never spoke to me again, avoiding me at all costs. I just can't imagine how a person who has chosen a career as a federal officer, especially a counselor, someone trained to help men adjust to prison and care for inmates, could be so cruel. It takes a heartless person to watch a sixty-year-old man, incarcerated for the first time, clearly suffering being away from his family, broken-hearted and crying, to lie instead of doing a simple part of the job she swore to do. Even with the number of times I begged her to help me talk to my wife, she just told me over and over, it wasn't permitted, yet that was a wicked lie.

I learned a few days later, when I was told by a different officer, that the long arm of the local prosecutor had reached Petersburg and instructions were given to restrict outside communication from me to anyone. This person said she believed it was to let whatever timeframe I had to file an appeal lapse before I could talk to an attorney. There is no way to prove this, but that's what I was told.

And later on, the "powers that be" did even more to block my freedoms. They continued their sick abuse of power. It was evil. There is no other explanation.

On day nineteen, when it looked like things might look up, my life took a dark turn for the worse.

9

THE VIRUS

*I am the way, the truth and the life. No one comes to
the Father except through me* (John 14:6).

After three weeks in prison, a whirlwind arrived in the block. A large outbreak of COVID-19 tore through the camp where I was headed, and they needed the cells we were in for infected inmates. The deputy warden strode in with his medical staff early in the morning and identified me as someone who could be released from quarantine that morning and transferred to the camp.

They told me to pack up, and all I could think about was perhaps that night, I could get on the phone and hear my wife's voice. I was so excited. They chained me at the waist and with handcuffs and ankle irons and walked me to another building. This was the first time I had been cuffed at all. Confusion set in because camp inmates don't get typically get cuffed, and it was a short distance to the camp. Did they think I would run for the barbed wire fence and try to escape? When I asked questions, the lieutenant, who I just met for the first time, got right up in my face and spit his words, telling me that asking questions was not permitted in prison if I wanted to have any comforts at all. The other inmates with us told me to be quiet or this guy would make life miserable for me.

As we walked outside, an officer holding a shotgun bigger than she was stood guard. My ongoing confusion and fear had me wanting to ask questions, but, of course, there was to be no communication. As I looked over at the camp, I saw multiple tents pitched outside and a refrigerated trailer. They herded us into a van and drove us not to the camp, but to the medium-secure facility's special housing unit. This is where inmates who get into trouble were sentenced to stay.

In prison, there are different classifications of inmates, and they cannot be mixed. They are minimum security (camp), which I was sentenced to, and then low, medium, and maximum security. This new unit was a barbaric place with smaller cells occupied by two men, and all of our privileges were taken, including phone (if you had it in the first place), email, outdoor recreation, newspapers, and more.

I couldn't help myself. Fear won out, and I asked the lieutenant why I was being taken there because the associate warden had told me I was going to the camp.

"It's for your safety."

The camp had over seventy infected inmates and was in lockdown—indefinitely.

"So you're taking me to the SHU [Special Housing Unit]?" My voice cracked. From the moment I was sentenced to this prison, people told me to avoid the SHU at any cost. "Don't worry. It's for non-punitive reasons, so you'll be OK," he lied. The transfer may have been for non-punitive reasons, but the restrictions were the same, as if I had committed a crime while in prison and was being punished. I was placed in a large holding cell, with no water and no toilet, mixed with guys there for punitive reasons and some for quarantine. I stayed in there for seventeen hours. I suffered dehydration because I'd had nothing to drink since the night before. The morning milk delivery was spoiled, and I was out of water bottles. I repeatedly asked for water and was ignored. When I asked about going to the bathroom, it took them two hours to get me a plastic urinal to use in public, in full view of all the officers, male and female, and other inmates coming and going. My urine was so dark, I asked for a medical tech. A physician's assistant arrived, and when I showed him the urine, he confirmed my dehydration.

His treatment? He came back with two paper four-ounce cups of water and told me that would hold me over. I couldn't believe it and grew angry. He was a licensed medical professional, and his answer to dehydration, which was now causing body cramps, was eight ounces of water. In other words, just enough to keep me alive.

I watched several inmates who were brought in fight with officers and be restrained. I listened as officers made fun of inmates who were crying or angry. I felt like I was in some other country, where humane treatment was non-existent.

Finally, one of the lieutenants sidled over. He told me they did not know what to do with me because of my minimum status and were working on sending me home or getting permission to put me in the population in the low-security section. He told me it would take about two days to work through, and then I would be able to leave and go somewhere other than there. He even tried to find a cell for me because he knew I had to be held alone and couldn't be mixed in with anyone there. Even camp-designated, minimum security inmates in the SHU could not be mixed with me because they were there for punitive reasons, and I was not. But the rules go out the window when they are tired of dealing with you.

The same lieutenant told me he had found a good spot for me, and they finally packed me up to go upstairs. Once an officer walked me to the new cell, I looked through the window and saw a medium-security inmate in the cell. The officer yelled out to the lieutenant, "We can't put him in here!"

Without another option, the lieutenant responded, "Put him in anyway. I am done. He'll be fine." The officer told me he didn't feel good about this because what they were doing was illegal. But he locked me in nonetheless. I don't mind admitting that I was not comfortable when I went in. These cells don't have bars; they have steel doors with small windows for looking into the hallway, two steel bunks, a toilet, a shower stall, and a tiny desk. Two guys have to live in this space for extended periods of time.

It turned out the guy in the cell was also in there only for quarantine as he had been outside the prison to see a doctor—not punitive reasons—and relief flooded me.

T-Rich, as he was called, told me he was sentenced to life and had been in prison for twenty years. *Sentenced to life.* In my mind, which was racing away, that meant he had nothing to lose. If I upset him, he could do anything he wanted to me, and it wouldn't—couldn't—add any time to his sentence. It felt unnerving, but I kept asking God for guidance and protection and a small measure of confidence that He was there returned.

After several hours getting to know T-Rich, my new "cellie" as they call it in prison, I felt much more comfortable. He was a good guy who hadn't been in trouble since he arriving in prison. And he knew the Lord and the Bible well, and we had a great talk about faith and trusting in the Lord. He told me the story about how he had also been targeted for crimes he did not commit and how a judge had stepped way outside his authority to sentence him to life when the maximum for his crime was ten years. (I think I know what you might be thinking: every inmate says they are innocent and have been treated poorly by the system, but as you read this, my friend T-Rich is close to becoming a free man, having been recommended for a writ of innocence by the attorney general in Virginia.) It took two decades to right the wrong because when police make mistakes, and prosecutors and judges go along to cover up those mistakes, it is hard to get anyone to listen. All the courts think about is if anyone can show that someone was falsely accused, falsely prosecuted, and imprisoned for crimes they did not commit, imagine how clogged the courts would be with appeals. So they fight you every step of the way to keep the truth from being heard.

The morning after my arrival to this cell, the morning-shift lieutenant peered through the window and asked me how I ended up in there. I told her what had happened the night before and she said, "This is not allowed. I will be right back." She never returned. (I can't make this stuff up!)

A counselor came to talk with me and said they had sent a request to the Court to have me moved to home confinement under the new CARES Act and were expecting an answer soon. The counselor repeated what others had said, that I should only be there a couple more days. I asked her about using the phone, and she said she'd look into it. I didn't hold my breath.

Then a miracle. Two days later, a guy showed up outside the cell with a piece of paper. I filled it out, and within two hours, I was on the phone with my wife! There are no words to describe my joy and relief. My tears mixed with my laughter as I listened to my family's voices for the first time in twenty-four days. Honestly, it renewed my anger at the first counselor over in the quarantine cell, the one who simply did not want to do her job. In my opinion, something evil lurks in people who intentionally hurt others.

Calls are only fifteen minutes long, but I was told we had 500 minutes per month and could make two calls per day. So when my first one ended, I waited the fifteen-minute required timeframe and called right back. What I didn't understand was that in the SHU, inmates are only allowed two fifteen-minute calls all month, not daily. That's part of their specific punishment, and even though I wasn't being punished, I was forced to live by the same rules because, according to one of the lieutenants, they didn't trust the staff to handle things correctly. He said if the phones were opened on the SHU for non-punitive inmates, officers would be tempted to accept payment from inmates to let others use them more too.

Several days went by with no communication at all from the staff regarding my transfer home. I woke up every day thinking they would just come get me and say your wife is here to pick you up. Sadly, the counselor finally came and said the prosecutor in my case objected to my release to home confinement, so they were working on getting the authorization to allow me to be housed in the low-security section or would have to transfer me to another facility. The counselor even asked me what I had done to that guy to [explicative] him off so much. This was the first time since they had started releasing people to home confinement that a prosecutor had filed such a harsh objection. I could not understand why he had so much anger toward me, other than perhaps he felt conviction because of what he had done to me.

So yet again, the prosecutor blocked a legal action, under the CARES Act, which was authorized by the US attorney general. No one should have that much power over another human being, particularly a prosecutor. Though, it is interesting that the people who often do wrong by us will avoid us at all costs. I continued to wonder how he had *any* power over a release that complied with the government's order and CARES Act. I assumed and maybe think even today that the prison and unbiased, independent judges should make these types of decisions to stay in compliance with federal orders. I communicated my thoughts, and the counselor laughed a little, telling me the system didn't work that way, as if I was a young child. Wardens and the courts work together. I felt sick. Knowing I had been targeted, charged, and convicted of crimes the government couldn't prove happened, knowing what he said at sentencing to send me away from my family to prison, and seeing how he was still doing everything he could to keep me locked up, even amid a global pandemic, I looked around, shaking my head at how his injustices had landed me illegally in the SHU. Next, I learned from a senior officer that the SHU is not allowed to be used for non-punitive holding, so they had reclassified me as a transfer inmate, one who now had to be in quarantine for fourteen days, even though I had been in quarantine already for thirty-one days.

Many of the prison guards told me to get my attorney involved. I remained polite, which the other inmates continued to tell me would get me nowhere, but I felt like it produced some empathy for my situation. The problem for me was I didn't have an attorney, certainly not one I could trust, and anytime I tried to notify the judge about what was going on, the courts reassigned the same public defender who had already proved her unwillingness to help me. At Petersburg, likely similar to all federal prisons, they do whatever they want and could use the pandemic as an excuse. Bottom line: the Bureau of Prisons answers to no one.

The SHU was an intimidating place, and I didn't know what to expect. I cried out to God. "Please hear my cries and rescue me from this, Lord. Help me before I have to be mixed in with men who have been incarcerated for many years, with different backgrounds than me."

The Lord brought me to Psalm 4, where David cries out to God to give him relief from his distress and have mercy on him. I was asking for the same. I believe our God is merciful to hear our prayers, and although He didn't answer the way I hoped, I lay my head down that night in peace, knowing He would provide for me, offering me opportunities to dwell in safety always. God wants us to put our trust in Him. If we rely on our own strength, we insult Him by making Him smaller, but when we trust Him, we become His chosen ones, whom He promises to hear when we call.

I remained locked in the six-by-nine cell with another man, with only a small toilet, sink, and shower stall. There were no windows, no access (not even a view) to the outside, and certainly no access to any news, live or on TV, day after day. I drew a calendar on paper to keep track of the days, which most guys in prison don't do. I understand how that environment can make men go crazy. Most officers were rude, bordering on inhumane, completely ignoring pleas for pain relief or medical visits. Spoiled milk was often served, and the response when people brought it up: *too bad.* The food was disgusting, mostly packaged sweets and sticky oatmeal, like what they might have served in the *Oliver Twist* story. In forty-two days, I lost thirty-five pounds–the most shocking and effective weight-loss program I had never signed up for.

Not every person was bad. There were some officers who tried to be kind, but frankly, those guards were often taken advantage of by guys who were so institutionalized, they were always up to something. I was amazed at the ingenuity of these guys. In each cell, there was a steel door and no way to get anything in or out unless an officer unlocked the small slot through which they slid food and supplies. So these guys developed a system where something flat but heavy, usually a package of tuna in a flat foil container, was tied to a long string made from strips of a sheet, sometimes as long as thirty feet, and slid under the doors with other things attached to them could pass items from cell to cell. At different times, I looked out the tiny window and saw bread, peanut butter packets, stamps, and other treasures moving from one cell to another. They would all work together to help each other out. Maybe you'd slide your item down the hall, and it wouldn't make it to the cell you wanted it to go to, so guys from another cell would push their own string system out to capture yours, then toss yours further down. You could move it as long as your string would go. The guy in my room had one over thirty feet long and had become a pro at sending stuff. Books of stamps are like money in prison, so if you were hungry, you could trade stamps for food just about any time. This system ended up being the only way I could write to my wife. I gave up food I wasn't going to eat anyway to get stamps. Most officers would help the guys trying to send things, especially if they were too big to slide under the door, but there were those who would see the strings and take them. It took most guys a day to make a new one, and the trading system continued.

I continued to ask daily for more phone use and eventually, one lieutenant let me go into his office and have a quick five-minute speakerphone call with my wife once a week. He was kind but still part of the system. He was pushing to get me out of the SHU, or at least to trustee status, but classification had me on hold to be transferred to another facility, though they assured me that would not happen. They just classified me that way to allow them to continue to hold me in the SHU, even as they told me they were still trying to get me home.

I later learned from someone who I will keep anonymous that they were not being honest and I would eventually be transferred to another facility. I finally met with a psychologist (something all new inmates in the SHU must do), and the doctor told me, "This is the most inhumane place I have ever seen. It makes me sick how they treat you guys, and I pray you don't need medical treatment because it is dangerous here." I had been complaining about cervical spine spasms that were causing me nerve pain in my arms and dizziness for over two weeks, but all of my requests to see a doctor were ignored. The psychologist told me my wife should start calling every day, demanding I be removed from the SHU, seen by a doctor, and afforded my rights under the CARES Act. The doctor also told me she should threaten to go to the media. She said that was the only way to get their attention, to get them to do what was right. My wife is not an intimidating type. She called every day, but they rarely answered and never put her through to anyone who could do anything. Promises for a return call were never kept.

I continued experiencing severe muscle spasms in my neck that caused tingling and numbness in my hands, and I requested to see a doctor daily for several weeks, but to no avail. I would fill out forms and submit them, but nothing. Sometimes, I would become so dizzy that I couldn't get off my bunk. My cellie asked everyone we saw to get me to the doctor, even an associate warden, who said he would be right back with a doctor. I don't have to tell you, but I will: That didn't happen.

One morning, I was taken to see the dentist for my initial check-up. I was so dizzy, I could barely walk, and my neck was in such spasms that my head looked off center on my body. The dentist was alarmed and took me by the hand to the doctor. She explained what was going on with me and asked the physician to see me. The doctor stepped into the room, looked at me, and refused to see me, saying she would get to me later in the week. The dentist and an officer standing there holding me were shocked, but the doctor walked away. One of them mentioned this was her typical response when it came to doing her job. He actually told me to request the other doctor by name because this one was so terrible.

I was in so much pain that all I could do was lay in the bed for days, mostly unable to eat, certainly unable to get up and stand. Both hands felt numb, but no matter how many different people we asked for help, we were ignored.

Eventually, someone took me to see the PA. When he saw me, he said, "You look like crap."

He noticed right away the spasms in my neck were so bad that my head looked as if it'd been shifted off my body. The tingling and numbness in my hands were spreading to my legs. When he saw that I had lost thirty-five pounds since I'd arrived, he was shocked. Though his words were only, "The SHU will do that to you." Then he laughed. My blood pressure was in the low nineties, which is good for a fifteen-year-old but not for a grown man. He commented it was unusual but not overly concerning. I asked him what he could give me to break the spasms.

"Ibuprofen."

"Give me a break. That's all you can do?" The psychologist had been right; medical care was dangerous here. He said he would put in an order for me to see a neurologist, but it would likely take three to four months. He said he would like to get some labs drawn on me, but no technician came to the clinic anymore because of COVID.

He left to consult with the physician, and when he returned, he said words than made me tremble with rage. "You really need to be seen at a hospital, but they won't let me send you."

He offered me a packet of ibuprofen and said, "Hope you feel better."

The officer who took me back to my cell told me to send in a daily request to see the doctor, but "request a specific doctor by name, not the one assigned here most of the week because she is dangerous and doesn't care." He confided that she had over one hundred malpractice lawsuits filed against her, but was protected by the prison system. I realize this is hearsay, not facts I can corroborate. So I will interject my opinion here. Doctors working in the prison system should not be employed by the prison. They must be free to make decisions that are in the best interests of the patients medically.

In late September, the lieutenant received the new transfer list for October and told me I wasn't going anywhere for at least another month. He told me to prepare myself to be there for the rest of the year because they weren't supposed to transfer anyone with the pandemic still a concern. I was so upset about this—the thought of five months in the SHU! He suggested I write a complaint to the chief counsel of the region about the lack of medical care and being held in the SHU. He thought that individual might have the power to do something to get me released to home confinement. The lieutenant gave me his name and mailing address. So that night, I wrote a complaint about everything that had happened: being held illegally in the SHU, the lack of medical care, being mixed with a medium-security inmate, and more. I sent it to my wife to be typed up and mailed out.

Here is the complaint letter my wife and I sent to the chief counsel. We received no response.

Michael Frazier
Regional Counsel Mid-Atlantic Region -
Bureau of Prisons
302 Sentinel Drive
Annapolis Junction, MD 20701
cc: Matthew Mallady, Regional Director

Dear Mr. Frazier,
    I was given your name and information by a senior officer at Petersburg Prison to share what is happening to me here.

    I self-surrendered to Petersburg Minimum Security Camp on July 29, 2022 to serve a 24-month sentence for wire fraud. I was held in a special quarantine unit in the Low building for 19 days. Prior to my arrival, I was told by the intake officer I would have access to phone and mailing materials the day I arrived. The same officer repeated that when I was booked into the prison. However, the counselor in the unit refused to get me the necessary code to use the phone, and I was unable to talk to my family for 24 days. When I finally spoke to an Assistant Warden, he could not understand why this had not been taken care of when I arrived, which was their usual protocol. It is clear the counselor simply did not want to do her job. Even shift supervisors in that unit assured me over and over they would make sure I was given the code to use the phone.

On August 19, two days prior to my move to the camp, a massive covid outbreak occurred, infecting dozens of inmates in the camp. They planned to move them into the cells we were in. I was told to pack up by an assistant warden who told me directly that I was going to the camp, but I was then chained and taken to the Medium SHU for "non-punitive" reasons. They told me it was for my safety. I was held in a holding cell with no running water or toilet facilities for 17 hours. The SHU Lieutenant told me they simply did not know what to do with me because I could not be mixed with other inmates due to my minimum status. He actually said they were working on finding a way to either get me sent home using the Cares Act or reclassify me to Low so I could go into population in that unit. He finally told me they had worked it out and I would only be there for two days. He had a cell for me to be alone and I was either going home under the cares act or to the Low building.

When an officer took me upstairs to the cell, he looked in the window and there was another inmate in there. He said "no way you can go in there with him" and yelled to the Lieutenant there was someone in the cell. He responded, "Just put him in there. He will be fine." The Officer was hesitant and told me to go in but this was not allowed. I met the guy in the call and learned he was a medium classified inmate serving his 21st year in prison and was sentenced to life. The next morning when the shift Lieutenant walked by she looked in and asked me how I ended up in that cell with him. A rhetorical question of course because she had to know I was put there. She said you can't stay in there, I will be right back. Never returned. Later in the shift she told me this wasn't right but they just didn't know what else to do. She even suggested I tell my attorney. It seems employees here do things they know are a violation of rules and my rights but feel they have no choice but to follow orders.

Over the past 5 weeks I have requested to be seen by a Doctor dozens of times, had Officers and even an assistant warden request medical for me only to be ignored. I am suffering from severe cervical spine muscle spasms causing numbness in both arms, dizziness and vision disturbances that prevent me from getting out of bed at times. Every nurse has been told about this and all they can offer is ibuprofen. They all state they are putting in requests to the Doctor for me as well as the forms I have completed.

When I was seen by a Dentist this week, she observed the severe spasms in my neck due to the alignment and walked me to see Dr [name removed]. The Dentist described my complaints, visual disturbances, dizziness and numbness. The Doctor walked out, looked at me and said "he's fine I will see him next week." The Dentist and Officer with me were both shocked and in fact asked her to see me now and she walked away. It has been 3 more weeks and I have filed multiple requests to be seen, a BP8 and still no response. A member of your medical team told me I should let my wife know and have her complain and get my attorney involved. She actually admitted "medical is so dangerous here and it is the most inhumane place I have ever been."

Additionally, although in here for non-punitive reasons, I have the same restrictions as someone in here for punishment. I am restricted to two 15 minute calls home per month, very limited commissary, no recreation, no sun, no windows, radio, television, etc. It has been 53 days now and I am being told I will likely be here in the SHU until after Christmas.

The culture here is terrible. The staff routinely state they hate it here, they have no respect for the leadership, the leadership talk about each other to inmates openly with disdain. They describe the warden as someone who "traded his humanity to climb the ladder." They admit they lie about the covid infections here because he insists he keep the number at zero even though it is clear it is not.

I have maintained my demeanor as calm and polite, respectful and obedient to the rules. There is no justification for keeping me in the SHU restricted as if I was being punished. I cannot tell you how many officers at all levels have advised me to contact an attorney to threaten to file a lawsuit because that is the only way to get anyone's attention. I chose this instead believing you will make sure policies are followed and I will be removed from here. I am clearly qualified for a [CARES] Act release to home confinement and was told that would happen then was told the Prosecutor objected and the prison goes along with that. What a system. I pray you will do what is right and remedy this situation without delay.

Sincerely yours,

Michael Morisi

The day after I sent it to my wife, around mid-morning, medical came by to do a covid test on me. I laughed because I had been in a cell for fifty-four days, but she told me I was leaving in four days. "To home?"

"New Jersey!"

"What?"

They really were transferring me to another prison, further away from my home? I demanded answers and was finally told by an officer that leadership had read my outgoing mail the night before, saw the complaint, and conferred with the regional director, who ordered me transferred out of his region before my wife had a chance to send the complaint to the counsel. That way, when it was received by their chief counsel, since I was no longer in their region, they would not be required to respond.

It absolutely appalled me. Four days later, on October 6, I was taken to see a PA and what we learned was besides losing thirty-five pounds, my vitals were well outside the normal ranges, and it was evident to him my neck was in severe spasms. He said, "You need to go to the hospital but they are transferring you tonight, so hang in there. I am sure the medical at Fort Dix is better, and I will call and let them know to see you upon arrival." He reiterated, "Medical here is dangerous." Seems everyone knew this fact, but no one did anything about it.

Later that night, at 2:30 a.m., three other guys who had either filed complaints or lawsuits and I were put in a forty-two-passenger bus with three officers and taken to Fort Dix, New Jersey. These men had been incarcerated for many years, so they came alongside me and helped me learn what was OK in prison and what could get me into trouble. We ended up becoming good friends.

When I first arrived in New Jersey, one of the senior officers told me if I wrote any letters there like I did at Petersburg, I would be transferred all over the country and never have contact with my family. I got the message.

There was some good news in all this. The medic I met upon arrival took one look at me, saw my neck spasms, and immediately requested permission to give me a shot to relieve them. He administered it, and within a day, I felt so much better. He said he would get me in to see a neurologist right away.

Several weeks went by, but no doctor visited. I learned no doctor visits were permitted while in quarantine. I asked for and got another injection because this guy was finally someone who cared. He wasn't a PA; he was a paramedic. I had been a paramedic for many years, so I think he was empathetic to my condition and story. Looking back, he was perhaps the first guy to really show that throughout the ordeal.

Despite treatment, my neck issues were getting worse by the day, affecting my vision. Life in this new facility was challenging. There was no heat, and thick black mold creeped everywhere. The windows didn't close completely, letting in the cold and new guys came in every day, which extended our quarantine period. (The officers always apologized for the "mistake" of bringing someone new in, but they still did it over and over.)

One afternoon, the word went out that we were all going to refuse our noon meal. I was hungry and not interested in participating in such a move but was quickly advised that, in prison, when a leader makes a decision like this, we all go along; otherwise, there are repercussions. So we all did. As an entire floor block, we refused lunch when the officers delivered it. Within an hour, several bosses and officers arrived to investigate what was going on. They do not condone such action, but in this case, there was little they could do because there were too many of us refusing to eat, and we were in quarantine. Right away, they wanted to know who was behind this. Of course, no one spoke up, so they listened to the demands of the group, which were listed on a paper, authored by someone who would never own up to it. And guess what? They met all of the demands! After all, they were pretty simple: coats, sweats (remember half the building had no heat and temperatures were in the teens), weekly laundry rather than monthly, two microwaves, and an extra phone (we had one shared between fifty men). I think the prison leadership made the right decision this time.

I was still suffering from severe neck pain, spasms, and headaches. Still experiencing numbness and tingling in my hands too. I continued to pray. My prayer was, of course, for the healing power of Jesus to cure my issues, but also that I would somehow be seen by a doctor who would take an interest in preventing the issue from getting worse and get me some relief.

God answered my prayers on October 26 while seated at a table playing cards. A severe pain filled my head and my vision went blurry, so I got up to walk to my room to lie down, but I collapsed on the way. I could barely see, and the pain in my head was worse than any migraine I had before. Medical came and interrogated me about what I had taken, what drugs I was using, etc. It's not the typical protocol for triaging a new patient, but this was prison.

I was moved by golf cart across the campus in freezing weather to the medical unit, where after an hour, a doctor finally appeared. I heard her call for an ambulance because she thought I may be having a stroke. Remember, I had been a paramedic for two decades. She had not performed a single stroke test, which all emergency professionals know when a stroke is suspected. I tried to explain the history of my problems, but everyone brushed me off. They called the ambulance, and we sat for another hour, waiting for officers who could go with me to the hospital.

Also remember, camp inmates do not require handcuffs or an officer to accompany them, but somehow, the prison had changed my status from minimum to low-security in the paperwork. Maybe it was so they could make it look like they were holding me in the right section. We may never know.

Once at the hospital, after several tests and specialized x-rays over two days, the physician came in and said she was keeping me a few more days to begin epidural injections to relieve the neck spasms. She had also scheduled a consult with the neurosurgeon for later that day to determine if cervical spine surgery was necessary. God had answered my prayer, but I didn't expect it to be this way.

Honestly, I was happy to be in a hospital and not the prison, where the doctors showed such indifference. The test results showed severe spasms with stenosis (narrowing of the nerve canals) in several spots in my cervical spine. About three hours went by. Then, with no more than an injection of a muscle reliever, the hospital staff came in to tell me they were releasing me.

What?! You heard that right.

The doctor told me the Bureau of Prisons had signed me out *against medical advice,* saying they would take care of me. I insisted they give me a copy of the discharge orders, which stated I needed an urgent neurosurgery consultation, some injections, and a couple prescriptions to break the spasms and help with the severe nerve pain.

Back at the prison, I was met by a lieutenant who took the discharge orders from me, saying, "We need these" even though they had their own copy. She assured me the doctor would see me the next day. I was thrown back in quarantine for fourteen more days, even though I was tested for covid before going to the hospital, upon arrival at the hospital, *and* before discharge from the hospital—all negative. I got back to my room and waited to hear from the doctor.

Over the next several days, I sent in requests to be seen and the officer working this new unit also requested medical care for me. Finally, after thirteen days, I was scheduled to see a physician's assistant (PA). She was very frank and told me she could only give me ibuprofen. "The doctor will never see you because if he did, he would be required to fulfill the discharge orders from the hospital," and I was too 'short-time' for them to invest in surgery and recovery time, especially during a pandemic. She went on about how medical protocols there were decided by non-clinical people and how dangerous it was. I believe she truly felt bad for me because she kept saying she could clearly see I had problems and was in pain. The spasms in my neck made my head look like it was pulled to one side, completely off center. I appreciated the honesty, but I was still flabbergasted they removed me from the hospital against medical advice and then refused to treat me as promised. The drugs the hospital had ordered (non-narcotic anti-spasm and nerve pain drugs) were not compliant with the Board of Prison's list of approved medications, so all I could get was, you guessed it, ibuprofen. Truly, again giving me those prescriptions acknowledges I have a problem…something they did not want to do in the record.

It'd been almost two months since I was discharged from the hospital, and I continued to suffer with cervical spine spasms. The numbness in my arms and now in one leg was worsening, and I hadn't seen a doctor. Most days, I was unable to walk the nearly quarter-mile to get meals, and they wouldn't allow another inmate to pick mine up. So they refuse to provide any medical treatment or food. This was when being friendly with the kitchen workers helped. I never went hungry. Many of the guys had been in for a while and seen this treatment of guys with medical issues, so they had empathy and brought me food. Unlike other inmates, kitchen workers were allowed to bring extra food out of the kitchen—or at least, they got away with it. These guys used this extra food to earn money, but never asked me for any money.

My personal doctor (who had reviewed my hospital records) and new attorney had both written to the warden, demanding attention, warning of the risk of permanent damage, but with no response. There was a cavalier attitude toward breaking the law by the very people who are charged with the care of people who broke the law. They do what they want, the way they want, with no accountability.

About a month or so later, the regional director's office wrote back and told my attorney I had seen a doctor at Fort Dix and was being treated for the problems and receiving good care. What a joke! I am not sure if he just felt good about telling a blatant lie or if the prison staff had lied to him, but either way, it was a lie.

Fortunately today, I have copies of my medical records, which clearly show it was a lie. In my eight months of incarceration, I never saw a physician, except for the brief stay I had at the hospital. I saw a nurse practitioner, who, as I stated, told me the doctor would not see me because the prison system didn't want to comply with the hospital discharge orders.

I was determined to get back to what God had for me to do. I was reading a book I had received (not knowing who sent it until I was released and learned it was my pastor, Bobby Hill) titled *David the Great*. It talks about the timing between the anointing and the announcement of our destiny and the fulfillment of it. It is a time of pruning to prepare us for His plans for us. That pruning includes lonely times (in caves for David), setbacks, and even doubts. David proved we should always do whatever God has us doing at the moment, even if we don't fully understand it. Or want it in our lives. We also must be careful not to make big mistakes by taking our eyes off of God, for distraction could damage our future. Don't try to force God's hand to move quicker and don't get ahead of Him. Through all of our struggles, keeping our eyes on Jesus, being a man after God's heart, is our only pathway to peace. I knew all of these things before entering prison's gates but was having a few problems understanding why all of this was happening to me.

10
THE CALL

---

*Therefore go and make disciples of all nations,
baptizing them in the name of the Father and of the
Son and of the Holy Spirit, and teaching them to obey
everything I have commanded you. And surely I am
with you always, to the very end of the age* (Matthew
28:19–20).

B ack on October 30, I received a devotional written by my
son. It was amazing, revealing a spiritual maturity he had
clearly developed over the past few months as he dealt with
my absence. Pride washed over me for him and his brother. My
wife shared that a teacher at our school had offered to minister
to my youngest son after school one day. That teacher later told
my wife she "cried her eyes out" because my son ended up min-

istering to her. She was amazed by his confidence in the Lord and the total trust he had in His plan for our family.

It was then I felt a prompting from the Lord to start a Bible study in my building. This floor housed fifty-two men, all in quarantine, most of whom had been in prison for many years or were back for the second or third times. High stress permeated the place, with so many strong attitudes weaving through it, and I felt like the Lord wanted me to usher in His presence.

We had two "game rooms" with tables where guys could play cards or dominoes, so I put up a sign in one of them, offering a Bible study the next night for 7:00 p.m. I also put some signs up in the TV room and hallways. Many of them were torn down, but I knew it would be OK. I was doing this because the Lord had asked me to.

The next night, I walked into the game room a little before seven. Guys played cards, so I sat in a corner on a ledge and opened my Bible. Suddenly, the guys all stood up and left. It was funny because you would've thought something pierced them. I sat there alone and read the Bible. Several men walked by and looked in the room, but no one came in.

The next day, I put up more signs advertising I was going to be there every night Monday–Friday at seven and on Sundays at eleven for church, so "come on in to study the Bible or for prayer!" The next night, again, I was alone.

But on the third night, three guys shuffled into the quiet room. And our time was amazing—beyond what I could have imagined. They were so broken yet shared openly about the pain they felt. Each one made a commitment to come every night to get to know Jesus better. I felt so close to Jesus because He allowed me to do this.

The same three guys showed up the next couple of nights. Then I was "summoned" by the associate of one of the toughest guys in prison, at least by reputation. He was a former gang leader from New York, and the message was that he wanted to talk to me privately. One of my cellies who had arrived from Petersburg with me was concerned for my safety. He gave me some advice about what to say and, more importantly, what not to say. But I felt a peace about the meeting, knowing God would be there with me.

I met the man in an empty room, and he asked me about the Bible study. I shared my heart for Jesus, answered his questions about faith and learned a lot about his life. We spoke for an hour or so before I asked him to join me that night in the Bible study. "I can't because the men in there last night are sex offenders. I can't mix with them." I was only then learning about the unwritten code of segregation that happens in prison: white, Black, Hispanic, sex offenders, and others. In prison, being a sex offender is a big issue. You are restricted by the other inmates from many places: TV rooms, lunch tables, and other places. They are often harassed.

"I don't ask anyone what they did. I just help them come to know Jesus," I told him.

The gang leader was curious about Jesus, so we talked about the commandments of Jesus to seek the Lord our God with all of our hearts, minds, souls, and strength and to love our neighbors as ourselves. I explained, "Jesus didn't say love those who never sinned or even those who are sex offenders or murderers. He said 'our neighbors,' which means everyone. We are all brothers in Christ." My words, prompted by God Himself moved this man. We talked and cried for over two hours, and by the end, he was crying out to Jesus for the first time in his life to forgive his crimes and behavior.

I sat amazed, watching the by-product of God entering that room and putting His arms around this guy. When we were done, I actually hugged him (which isn't done in prison), and he said that was the first time a man had ever hugged him. That really broke my heart to hear and opened my eyes to what so many of these men face growing up in fatherless homes, their only influences being men involved in crimes or who want something from them.

That same night, this man, with the reputation of violence and a position of power, came into the Bible study with the three men he had previously shunned and apologized to them for the abuse they had endured—some of it by him—and called them his new friends. My heart shook as I watched them interact with each other. Those men were thrilled that someone of this leader's reputation was actually calling them friends. The only thing I said the entire evening was, "God loves us all equally. He doesn't love us any less because of what we have done." They took it from there.

The next night, eight guys showed up because word had spread about what was happening in that room. Some came and sat quietly and listened. Some spoke, and others spoke a lot, opening up and sharing their fears, regrets, as well as their dreams for life after prison. God was moving in that place, and it was a privilege for me to witness.

Much like the first church in Acts, night after night, the gathering grew. During the days, several of the men would request one-on-one time with me. I saw Bibles opened in cells and conversations going on around what people were reading.

Then one officer told me what I was doing wasn't permitted. *What?*

The new peace enveloping the floor was so evident, you would have assumed the prison staff would have appreciated it, even wanted it. But no.

The officer told me Christians were not permitted to lead other Christians in gatherings. "How is it that the Muslims gather five times per day to pray—quite loudly—and the Board of Prisons dictates we honor them, even threatening disciplinary action for interfering with them, but Christians can't gather?" I boldly explained to the officer that God had told me to start the Bible studies, so I was just going to keep doing it until someone officially made me stop.

"Suit yourself."

Over the next few weeks, many guys were released to the general population, and we were down to sixteen of us in quarantine. I had only two days left, so it came as no surprise when they brought two new guys onto the floor, which meant, yep, we all had to start our fourteen days in isolation all over again.

Next, the prison staff moved all eighteen of us to the first floor, which had only one bathroom, one shower, and one television. We were forced to live doubled and tripled up in seven rooms. This floor had a severe case of mold, and, again, we were told not to drink the water. The conditions were horrendous.

Every night, guards braved coming onto our floor with devices to ensure no one had a cell phone. The officer told us they were afraid someone would sneak one in and take pictures of the walls, the mold, and the general conditions and send them out. They couldn't allow that to happen.

Somehow, these eighteen guys made it all work. There were some arguments, but no fights broke out, and we all remained respectful of each other. The best part was that we managed the use of one toilet and one shower with no problems—a true miracle.

Finally, quarantine ended, and it was time to move into the general population. Of course, the question about me moving to the camp (minimum security) was, once again, passed over.

The process to move us was crazy, at least to me. Inside a fenced yard, with razor wire everywhere and armed guards stationed at key points, they still chained us at the waist, hands, and ankles, simply to ride a bus 500 yards. Then, they unchained us and let us walk a couple of blocks to our building. It's all about control and making sure you know you have no freedom.

I walked into my new room where five other guys were and dropped my stuff by the bed I was assigned. One of the guys spoke. "Don't unpack until I see your papers." I had been told this would might happen, so I was prepared. The inmate was asking for my court records of my case to ensure I wasn't a sex offender or a snitch. What I learned was that if either of those charges were in my records, they would order me out of the room, which would mean I'd have to see the officer and request the SHU! There is a fine line regarding who controls the prisons.

My new cellie read my charges and sentences to everyone, and they were happy with my papers, so I was allowed to unpack. The five other men had served sentences ranging from nine years to twenty-six years, so I was in unfamiliar territory, but I had Jesus with me so had no concerns. As always, I showed respect and kindness to everyone. I made the decision that the only thing they would see from me was the love they were unaccustomed to and a kindness not displayed by many in prison. I wanted them to see Jesus in me, even if they didn't know it was Him.

Every room I walked into for the next few weeks was met with the same request: We need to see your papers. I carried them with me every day. In this building of about 300 men, we had five television rooms, one for Black guys, one for white guys, one for New York guys, one for Latinos, and one that aired exclusively sports . . . so everyone was in there. The room for white guys had to take the sex offenders who were relegated to row five and behind. In that room, if you had clean papers you could sit in the first four rows; otherwise, you could stand in the back. It did not take long before I was welcomed in all the rooms. Though no one could understand it because most were exclusively race focused.

I was the only white guy in the Black or Latino TV rooms, the only white guy allowed to sit at their lunch table (they were segregated too), and I was the only white guy allowed into many other rooms, regardless of the room's leadership or race designation. All I did was talk about Jesus.

There was one Bible study meeting one night per week, so I jumped in. The guys in my room were quick to tell me it was run by sex offenders, and they didn't want me in there. But, I never asked about their crimes, and it became a non-issue once they knew I was going to continue attending.

After about a week there, I finally met with my counselor. She asked me about moving to the camp since I was camp designated, which I really wanted to do, based on all I had heard about the freedoms the inmates there get. However, she suggested I may be a lot happier in this building. I guess the camp was a former aircraft hangar with 185 guys all sleeping in bunk beds in one area, and the environment often caused the men to get into more trouble than they did where I was staying.

I felt like the Lord prompting me to stay put. He had work for me to do and revealed it soon after making this decision, prompted in large part by my wife's faith.

———

Praise to God, I was permitted to talk to my wife and boys every day, and it made such a difference for my family and me. Each day, my wife's first question was, "Where did you see God's glory show up today?"

I would usually respond, "His glory isn't here." Though I was reading the Bible every day and soaking in every word, clearly saw Him work in the men's lives, and knew He was working in mine, I still held onto some frustration about being in prison at all. I knew in my heart the Lord was there, but I fought the whole situation that my family and I were being forced to endure. My heart was angry with the people who had done this to us. I harbored an epic grudge.

Despite starting every morning and finishing every night reading the Bible, and though I had books to read every day that drew me closer to God, I struggled with unforgiveness. I loved reading His Word and looked forward to it. I especially appreciated the books my wife sent me; they were a great source of strength. One book I read was *The Veil* by Blake Healey. He is the lead pastor for Bethel Atlanta and also leads the School of Supernatural Ministry. This book was amazing; I could not put it down. It opened my eyes to the spiritual realm, the one we have the opportunity to experience each day, and I decided that was where I wanted to live. I ended up reading his two follow-up books called *Profound Good* and *Invincible*. All were equally engaging, and I have read them now a couple of times each.

They helped me put aside my earthly vision and see with God's eyes. As I walked around the building, I kept my mind centered on the visions Blake had talked about in *The Veil*. I wanted to see the spiritual realm at work.

On November 19 (I'll never forget the date), everything changed for me. On that day's call, my wife asked me where I had seen God's glory. I told her again I didn't but decided that day, I would ask God to show me His glory. To truly let me live out my faith and trust in Him. I asked God for His light to shine in me so brightly that everyone would notice. I told Him I wanted to see His glory so I could answer my wife when she asked me the next day. I wanted to see these men the way He does.

And wow, did He come through. I woke up feeling great that morning, with a clarity I had not had before, and finally realized there was a divine purpose for me being unjustly imprisoned.

I promised God that I would boldly proclaim who He was to everyone I came in contact with and asked Him if He would stay with me, protecting me. What transpired was nothing short of miraculous. As my path crossed with others that morning, men I had seen every day, I suddenly saw them differently. I could see their pain, their regret, and their shame as I looked into their eyes. I saw little boys in men's bodies, fighting to secure some obscure identity in prison, even identifying themselves as prisoners, instead of seeing themselves as Christ saw them. I determined I was going to make sure every one of them knew how much God loved them.

I can't describe what this surrender to God's call felt like to me. I imagine you have to experience it for yourself, but it is a freedom and peace unlike anything the world can give you, no matter how much money or fame you have.

I walked differently that day because I walked with the authority and confidence of not only knowing God was there, but *feeling* Him beside me. Others noticed my transformation. Scores of guys asked me what had changed.

"Did you cut your hair?"

"Didn't you have a beard before?"

They knew something was different but couldn't figure out what it was. I proudly told them it was Jesus inside me they saw. Many rolled their eyes. Others simply walked away, but I knew a seed had been planted.

As I reflected on my time in prison to that point, I could see what God wanted me to learn about me and how I could truly engage in an intimate relationship with Him. I believed I had been seeking God's heart for many years, but the clarity I now had made me wonder if I was seeking it to glorify Him or for my own benefit. I had been incarcerated for ninety-seven days, and it had been the hardest days of my life for many reasons—mostly being away from my family—but also, I realized, it had been the best time growing closer to God. He had shown me things, told me things, and taught me things beyond anything I could have imagined, and I knew our relationship would continue to grow deeper.

I understood I had been called for a specific purpose: to evangelize the authentic gospel of Christ to as many people as possible, to those who society had tossed away, along with the key to their physical freedom. And I realized, *I get to do this every day I'm here and can't wait to see how He will use me when I am free.*

I had been invited to lead one night of the Bible Study. I felt strongly we needed more and I changed it to five nights a week. The chaplain wasn't happy that I did that without his permission (I didn't mean to take charge but didn't even know there was an established leader!). He did not think it was wise, but we did it anyway. Sometimes, it's meaningful when leadership comes from within, and before long, we had twenty to twenty-five guys attending every night. We also held church services on Sunday in the building, which saw close to double those numbers at times. It was a beautiful testament to God's sovereignty. I take no glory for anything that happened; God gets all the glory.

I would like to believe I brought the confidence and authority that Jesus has, and the truth that all any of us are called to do is glorify Him, so that's what I wanted to do. I met some passionate lovers of Jesus who knew the Bible and were very gifted singers, preachers, and teachers. My goal was to help them identify those gifts and recognize Who gave them to them and they could proudly represent Jesus every day. Again, I got invited to pray with and share with some of the toughest guys in prison who ended up learning and accepting Who they were in God's eyes. Most of them initially had a hard time understanding they are all sons of God and believing how much He loves them, even in their filth. I talked to them about how living separated from Him is a recipe for a life of struggle and disappointment.

I told these guys they had a choice to make, to let all of the bad things they had experienced in their lives become their identity (and future) *or* believe every word God says and seek Him daily, finding peace amid the struggles and challenges. Many thought they had to get cleaned up before they could turn to God. I shared with them that they could never clean up enough to give them access to God. They had His love and desire for relationship because of the blood of Jesus, shed on the cross for them, and His resurrection from the grave.

Many heard this, the Good News, for the first time, and it changed their attitudes and perspectives. All over the building, the prison experienced less anger and fewer fights. Instead, Guys opened their Bibles, attended studies and services, and asked for prayer about things going on with their families on the outside. I felt humbled when guys asked me to talk to their moms or family members on the phone, and I heard their cries of joy because their son, their dad, their brother had been changed. More peace.

God never promises us that life will be smooth and easy. He says, "No weapon forged against you will prevail, and you will refute every tongue that accuses you . . ." (Isaiah 54:17). What this makes clear is weapons will be formed against us, and things won't go as we plan. But throughout those challenges, God does promise us peace and comfort if we know He is in control and loves us with an unconditional love that we can't fully understand. Once we get a real revelation of who He is and how much He loves us, being with Him becomes our goal every day.

I will be forever grateful for what God did through me. One of the guys in my room told me that in the sixteen years he'd been in prison, he had never seen anyone have so much access to men of every race and background. And he wondered why it was happening then. I tried to help him understand it was the grace of Jesus, but he was a Muslim and not convinced. Over six months of living in the same room, watching me pray, read the Bible, lead studies, and hold Sunday worship with some of the toughest guys in there, it never got to his heart that Jesus is Lord. Many people have a hard time breaking the beliefs they've held for their entire lives, even if those beliefs never brought them the peace and comfort and direction a relationship with Jesus promises.

This man will probably be out of prison by the time this book is published, and I pray he opens his heart to welcome Jesus in. I know it will change his life. He is a good guy with tons of gifts, which I believe the Lord intends to use for His glory. I pray for him often. He had been incarcerated since the age of eighteen. His story is a familiar one—a young boy, raised on the streets, no dad or mom, who became a drug runner for a dealer and grew up quickly to become a boss. He had carried a gun since fourteen, shot two people in a rage at seventeen, and ended up in federal prison for twenty-four years. Society and the system had failed him. Washington, DC, failed him, and he had become just another statistic, growing up in federal prison.

Another guy I met was convicted of bank robbery and sent to prison, where he had an affair with a federal officer, which got him more years and a trip to the maximum-security prison. As a young man, they sent him to a place where people are stabbed daily, fights and weapons are commonplace, and you do whatever is necessary to survive. Again, a broken man entered a broken system; he was not managed properly, given the responsibility they have for rehabilitation.

———

New guys came to our prison every day, some self-surrendering to a prison full of COVID-19, to be locked down in a quarantine building with no access to outside recreation or sunshine, limited commissary, no programs or services, and many of them first-timers in prison. Many of them had committed non-violent crimes that could easily be punished through home confinement or halfway houses. I watched them experience the same emotions—worry, concern, fear—I did, and I did my best to assure them God was with them, loved them deeply, and would help them every step of the process if they would just surrender to Him.

Although I was humbled to share Jesus with these men, I still suffered, praying every day that God would send me home to be with my family. As the holidays got closer, the despair in my boys' voices as they begged God to get me home before Thanksgiving broke my heart. I begged for the same and hated they had to go through this. In the end, I told them, we would all come out stronger. My wife also wanted me home, but her faith and trust in God and His timing was unbelievable. She is a rock when it comes to her faith. Unwavering.

My Day 100 journal entry: "Just hung up with Shannon [my wife], and my heart is shattered. Dominic sounded numb, and Danny was crying so hard he couldn't even talk or be consoled. I guess the emotional toll this is taking hit a low today. Why God? What more can you possibly have for me to do here that warrants my family falling apart, broken-hearted? Only you can bring healing by bringing us all back together. Please Father, forgive my questioning You, but I am a wreck and want to go home to my family. We want to be together and the pain for my family, including my eighty-year-old father-in-law, has gone on long enough. My family loves you and serves you daily; we pray to you daily and seek your heart, yet here I sit, and we are all broken-hearted. Hear our cries for your mercy and send me home, Lord. Do it supernaturally so only you can get the glory for it. We will sing your praises."

Still, I remained. Our nightly Bible studies were going well and more and more men were coming to me privately to learn more about Jesus. It was a blessing to see so many yearning to know and understand who God is. For the most part, most of the men I met in prison had never been exposed to Jesus, had never experienced such genuine love. Some followed the Muslim faith—many because it was what most do in federal prison, but they found nothing in it to inspire them. They were inspired by Jesus and all He did for us, but mostly, they were inspired to know He is alive and still loves them and craves a relationship with them.

In a conversation with one man, I learned he was convinced he would get the chance to stand before God and negotiate his way into Heaven. He planned to tell God all the ways He let him down and believed God would see him as a good person and be flexible. This is just a way to say you believe in God, Heaven, and Hell but live your life the way you want, believing it's good enough to spend eternity with Jesus. This man does not believe Jesus is the Messiah, nor does he believe Jesus died and was resurrected. As encouragement to him, I shared the words of Jesus in John 14:6: "I am the way, the truth and the life. No one comes to the Father except through me."

11

MY SINGLE DESIRE

To this you were called, because Christ suffered
for you, leaving you an example, that you should
follow in his steps (1 Peter 2:21).

My daily prayer was that I wanted to see with His eyes, hear with His ears, and feel and love with His heart. I committed to speak only what I heard Him say, to want only what He wanted. And night after night, the gathering grew. During the daytime, several of the guys would want private time with me, so I would introduce them to Him. My goal was that long after I was gone, they would still seek to spend time with Jesus.

One morning, a friend from quarantine arrived, and I wanted to see him, so I knocked twice on the door to his room and then walked in. I had become comfortable doing so, and no one seemed to have an issue with it. That day was different. There were seven guys in this room, with one of them clearly heralded as the boss. I would soon learn this New York guy was highly regarded all over the prison as "the boss." And when I walked into his room that day, he made it clear, if I ever did that again, he would punish me and in ways that didn't sound good to me. I won't give you the details, but I got the message.

I immediately apologized for my misunderstanding and assured him he would not have to worry about me making that mistake again. I walked out as his threats followed me, to make sure I didn't forget.

Shortly after, he came into a computer room and summoned me back to his room. Fear grabbed me as I wondered what he was going to do, but I had become so certain God was with me and protecting me that I walked in with authority (not my own). All the same guys were there, and I truly thought I was going to suffer my first beating. The boss sat in his chair and apologized to me, acknowledging he didn't know I was a man of God and was sorry he had offended me because he felt that was an offense to God.

What?!

I couldn't believe my ears, but my heart praised Jesus. The boss went on to ask for my forgiveness and said I was welcome in his room anytime. I prayed—right then, right there—with him and the rest of the guys and told him how much God honored him for doing what he had just done. He was clearly moved. Over the next few months, John and I prayed together often— anytime the Lord prompted me, I showed up and asked him if I could pray for him. He shared a lot with me, and since leaving prison, I have maintained some contact with his family. I learned from his sister (just a few days ago from the time of this writing) that he was released and is home, and I could not be happier. I know how much he wanted to be with his family. I still pray for him often and hope to connect with him again soon.

Sometime soon after, a friend came to tell me that Virginia and New York were going to battle. In prison, the state you are from becomes your prison family, and if the order is given by a "shot-caller" to go to battle with another state, you must join and fight or risk being punished by your own state for not helping. This particular guy told me that members from both New York and Virginia knew I was not involved in this dispute and would excuse me when it went down. Some part of me believes it was my new friend, the boss from New York, who excused me. God is so amazing with how He works to set things in motion, things we don't often see until much later. This runner, or messenger, said he would give me the cue and wanted me to go to my room and stay there until he let me know it was safe. He said it was going to be bloody.

My heart ached, and I was uncomfortable with the whole thing, worried about some friends I had made who could get hurt . . . or worse. Tensions were high on the floor, and everyone could feel something was up. There was lots of talk about making sure "you had your knife with you at all times." (I never carried one.) For the next two days, I prayed non-stop that God would intervene and stop the fight before anyone got hurt. I did not want to see that happen. I walked the halls with my arms outstretched, asking God to pour His Spirit into every man and to send angels of protection to us.

And God answered the prayer as we hoped.

I finally got word the dispute had been settled peacefully, and there would be no war. Praise Jesus!

Our nightly Bible studies were going well and more men sought me for private meetings to learn more about Jesus. My spirit soared to see so many yearning to know and understand who God is.

It is a strangely empowering feeling to go through this type of challenge—to be incarcerated for a crime that never happened, targeted by a broken and corrupt system, treated poorly by fellow Americans, and be transferred in retaliation to a place my family could not visit, with COVID-19 running rampant in the prison, and mistreatment, poor food, dirty water and moldy conditions . . . yet walk it out with the indescribable peace that God was with me. I learned worry does nothing. And I became anxious about nothing. I yearned for the comfort of being with my family, but there, in prison, I was, serving God for His purposes. That is a message I was determined to share to everyone: Worry will not change the outcome, and the only source of peace is Jesus.

———

Also during this time, the conditions of the prison scared me more and more. These buildings had been condemned, empty for years before the BOP decided to use them for inmates. In the first building I stayed, as I mentioned, the black mold was so thick, it appeared to be alive. The officer there told us he was made to sign a waiver preventing him from holding the prison responsible for health problems he may or may not develop while working in there. They told him to wear a mask, and this was before masks were a thing due to coronavirus.

In the population building I was moved to, a trustee was tasked with walking around daily with a paint brush, covering any place the mold was oozing through the paint. It was terrible. The rusty pipes were just as bad, and the water on some days would smell like the sewer and then later in the day like a chlorinated pool. We knew what they were doing to cover up the filthy water: adding chlorine. We didn't drink the water. I learned quickly to get bowls of ice (the ice machine had a filter on it), then get bottles of the 180-degree water we used to cook with and mix them. Once the ice melted, the water became room temperature and you could drink it pretty confidently.

With the billions of dollars states provide to the BOP every year, they could at least provide sanitary conditions for the men and women they are responsible for, including clean food and water.

It had also become clear the BOP had no idea how to handle the COVID-19 outbreak. They seemed to shoot from the hip, with no strategy or definitive plan. It was clear that people with no clinical experience were making the decisions. Even the medical staff openly spoke about the terrible way it was being handled. It's an uneasy feeling to know the people you are dependent on for everything you need are incapable of planning for tomorrow, much less developing a strategy for handling a long-term pandemic challenge.

In our building, 284 men tested positive for the virus. It took five days for the test results to come back, and sixteen men tested negative. So anyone with any common sense at all would know those sixteen men were also exposed, but they separated all of us, put those men on the ground floor alone, and locked 284 men on the top two floors for two weeks. This enraged many of the guys because it was not a comfortable environment. Everyone was on edge, so I just kept trying to share the love of Jesus on our floor. Of course, as soon as our two weeks were almost up, the seventeen tested positive, and they moved them to our floors, which extended our lock down once again.

All 284 men were now mixed with the seventeen COVID-19 positive guys, and although there was no way for us to get reinfected (that we knew of), they kept us all isolated, locked down on our floors. By the end, 300 men got COVID-19 in our building, but only three were sick. Those three were over 300 pounds each and suffered from pneumonia. They were sent to the hospital and after they "fully recovered," were back within three days. You barely heard a cough in our building. Most of us lost our ability to taste and smell. Over a couple-month period, nearly 2,200 men ranging from twenty-two to eighty-seven years old, with various health issues, were positive for COVID-19, and all fully recovered.

Nonetheless, I felt peace because God was with us. Not just with me, but with all of us. What I came to realize through all this was that it was God's job to fight. It's always His job to do the fighting. Our job is to trust in Him—just trust, not question or try to yank the steering wheel from His hands. Pray, then wait and watch Him get to work. That's surrender. That is where peace comes.

Sunday mornings in prison were both the best and toughest for me. They were the best because it was quiet. Most guys slept late. And the best day because we have church service. Most guys spend the afternoons watching football, so I found more quiet time alone, without distractions, with the Lord. All I wanted to do every day was read the Bible, reflect on what I read, talk to Jesus, then listen for His voice to respond.

But Sundays were the worst days, too, because traditionally, they were such a great family day at home, and I wanted to be there so badly. On Sundays, we would have breakfast together, go to church, and often head out to lunch afterward. I usually cooked on Sundays, and it was always a peaceful, nice day for our family. We relaxed after dinner and got to sleep early to kick off the new week with loads of energy. I loved those days and missed my family so much.

12

PRAYER WALKS

Do not be anxious about anything, but in every
situation, by prayer and petition, with thanksgiving,
present your requests to God. And the peace of God,
which transcends all understanding, will guard your
hearts and your minds in Christ Jesus
(Philippians 4:6–7).

everal guys approached me over the next few days to talk about my prayer walks. They noticed me pacing the building, talking with God. Questions from guys who had never heard of such faith. From one end of our building to another and back twenty times equaled one mile. I logged many miles talking to God in that building. A few asked me right out if I had prayed about the war that was planned inside the prison walls, and I gave God all the glory for it not happening. There is nothing the enemy throws at us that cannot be overturned or rejected by the strength and power of Christ if we would just tap into it. God gave us the same power we read in the Bible—the power Jesus used—but it takes great faith and total surrender to see that power in action.

I was so close to Jesus now and had such trust and confidence in Him. I counted every thought as His. A week before Christmas, I was praying unceasingly that I would get to surprise my family for Christmastime at home. I just knew God was going to move mightily and in ways only He could, to get the glory. I could not imagine Him letting my boys suffer through this wonderful holiday, the one that celebrates Jesus's birth, without me.

One night a snowstorm arrived. I wasn't expecting it because I rarely watched TV. The heartbreaking thing about that snowfall for me was that I had been certain I was heading home, but if it snows, even if inmates are scheduled to be released, the prison cancels them when it snows. That morning after the snowstorm, I didn't have a normal quiet time with Jesus. I was upset with Him and just didn't feel like talking.

I stood alone in my room, which was unusual, looking out of the window at the grounds, staring at the fences and the razor wire around them, thinking about how ugly that prison was. Feeling sorry for myself, I suppose. As I continued to peer outside, a beautiful red cardinal landed in a tree just outside the window and simply perched there. At that instant, I felt the love of God in a way I never had. Oh, I always knew He loved me, but I felt it deep in my heart, His loving embrace that told me He saw me, and suddenly, all I noticed was beauty. I was in awe that God could make a snow-covered prison yard look so stunning. It gave me peace.

In federal prison, inmates may not gather together as Christians outside of the chapel. Well, the chapel was closed because of COVID-19, so our nightly Bible studies continued to grow as did our Sunday services. More than once, guards came in and randomly searched several of the guys sitting in the room where we held our Bible studies. The guards repeatedly told me I couldn't do this, gather others to study the Bible.

Their warnings turned into verbal threats. "You could lose good time or be sent to the SHU (a.k.a., the hole)." I explained that God had asked me to do it, and then they'd walk away.

There were several others leading these services, too, but I guess I had a high profile because I walked every day with Jesus. Literally. In the book of Acts, in Chapter 4, Peter tells the rulers of Jerusalem, "Which is right in God's eyes: to listen to you, or to Him? You be the judges! As for me, I cannot help speaking about what I have seen and heard walking with Jesus" (verse 19). I feel the same way. There is no doubt in my mind; He walked every step with me, slept alongside me, and was there when I woke up every day.

Finally, one morning, a supervisor told me to keep doing what we were doing and not to worry about anything happening to us. He could clearly see the positive impact the Bible studies were having inside the building. God was so good to us.

As I was preparing for one of the studies, the Lord spoke to me and told me to pray for someone named Michael because he had a twisted spastic colon and had been in pain for many months. I knew we had three guys named Mike, so before we got started that evening, I asked which Mike had this condition. One raised his hand, so I gathered all the men together to lay hands on him and prayed fervently that the work of the enemy to cause this problem in this temple of God, this man of God, to leave and for God to fully restore his body. This was something most of these men had never seen or experienced, and many were skeptical. Mike simply sat down and didn't say much.

It wasn't until several weeks later that he confessed to the group he had not experienced any pain or discomfort from the condition since we had prayed. He had been healed. Mike is a good man and is now out of prison, living in Baltimore and working. He has connected with a church where a good friend of mine is the pastor and we talk often. God is always so good!

I became even more known across the building as the "Jesus guy." I liked that title because if I had to be in prison at all, I wanted to do everything possible to glorify Him. I continued my prayer walks.

Believe it or not, cooking in prison is an art and if someone cooks for you, it's an honor. So in the midst of the segregated environment I referenced earlier, the Hispanic guys are quite talented cooks. Cooking was accomplished through one of two methods—with a "stinger" or an iron.

A stinger is an extension cord with the plug cut off. Then the wires are attached to something metal, which is dropped into a bucket of water, where bags of rice mixed with all kinds of meats, cheeses, and sauces are combined with seasonings and boiled for thirty minutes or so. What comes out is really delicious.

Another thing we cooked with is a standard household clothing iron. I became quite a pro at filling burritos with the same rice, meats, cheeses, and seasonings, rolling them up tightly, then taking them to the "Iron Grill," run by a guy named "ATL" (everyone in prison has a nickname). He had two irons he used to cook any burrito for a dollar, paid for with stamps (prison currency).

I kept him busy cooking burritos at least three times per week. Several guys brought me the ingredients to make the burritos, and in return, I could eat one. Some of these guys were so good, they learned to use anything we could buy in the commissary to prepare a meal fit to be sold in any restaurant. I told ATL when we got out that he should open a restaurant in Atlanta called The Iron Grill and actually use irons to cook the sandwiches and burritos. Hope he does that one day. He would do well.

"ATL" joined our Bible studies as often as he could, but cooking for the floor was his source of income and the studies happened at a time when he was typically very busy. Guys eat late in prison but also because the guards develop a schedule of walking around and right after dinner, you were pretty safe to do whatever you wanted until the 9:30 p.m. head count when we all had to be standing by our beds. Counts happened twice a day during the entire week, with an early morning one on weekends. An extra guard always came over for counts; but otherwise, we had three floors, 300 men, and one guard who may walk the floor once or twice during a twelve-hour shift—if that.

Cooking with stingers or irons was not a permitted activity. They knew it happened (who can't smell it!), but if they actually caught you, depending on the guard, sometimes you got into trouble, or more often, you'd get lucky, and he or she would just let it go.

Many of the guys on the floor took part in other non-permitted behaviors. They either had cell phones, which they rented by the hour, or sold marijuana, tobacco cigarettes, or alcohol, and they would pay look-outs to keep their activities under the radar. Look-outs would earn up to $100 per week for standing guard at the top of the stairs and calling out when they heard a guard approaching or saw the compound officers coming.

When the compound officers came, we knew rooms were going to be searched. It was really an amazing system, and I believe many of the guys who ran businesses inside could be very successful outside prison in legitimate entrepreneurship. They had ingenuity and strategic planning abilities that rivaled most business professionals.

———

Christmas came and went, and I was still in prison, and still seeing God move every day ans he revealed His glory to me and through me to others. In February, the prison system announced "mandatory" vaccinations, with loopholes. As they questioned us about who wanted to take it and who didn't, so many were planning to refuse that they came up with a plan. They planned to isolate those who refused the vaccine in a single building, with no access to recreation or outside time. These men would be essentially locked down in quarantine until the pandemic was over, and by that time, it seemed the government had no intention of ending the pandemic.

I planned to refuse the vaccine. Remember, we had all contracted COVID-19 already, and none of us got really sick. The news reports we were seeing told us the unvaccinated were the ones being treated in hospitals and dying. It made me wonder if it was covid killing them or the treatment they were receiving. I just didn't trust the vaccine, nor believed it was necessary. My faith in how God created our immune systems was enough.

It was mid-March and I was told when our building was scheduled to get the first shot, I would have to "officially" refuse it then, with the nurse, and sign something. So I was prepared.

Unknown to me, God was busy working on a plan, which He was about to unveil.

I woke up the morning of the vaccination appointment with a swollen tonsil, nearly twice its size, so clearly, I was fighting some kind of viral infection. It was evident when I looked in my throat. When I got to the gym area to refuse the vaccine, I told the nurse about my tonsil, and she looked at it. Because it was clear I had some kind of infection, I could not get the vaccine anyway so did not have to "officially refuse it." I was disqualified at that time.

The non-clinical medical director was there, as well, so besides sharing all of the problems I had endured over the past five months with my neck spasms and hospital discharge, which he said "shocked" him, (I am pretty sure he was spinning me), I told him about my tonsil. He ordered someone to see me right away. He also assured me a doctor would see me about my cervical spine spasms and the treatment I still needed. Hope grew that maybe some relief was on its way.

I was scheduled the next day with a nurse practitioner. She believed it was something viral which made sense to me as well. She instructed me to watch my swollen tonsil for seven to ten days, and if it wasn't down to return to the clinic.

Twelve days later, I finally got in to see her. It was no better. As a former paramedic, I knew a viral infection would not last over twelve days, so I assumed it had to be bacterial. The nurse practitioner agreed, however she refused to treat it.

I insisted that I be seen by a physician immediately. I wanted antibiotics because if it was a bacterial infection, it would just get worse if left untreated. She left the room, and when she returned, she simply refused. "You'll be fine." I grew really concerned.

The next morning is when God fully revealed His plan. My counselor called me to her office.

"You're going home in six days."

I could not believe what I was hearing. I was not set to be released until September 16, more than five months away, but she was telling me I could leave April 8.

Praise Jesus! He did it!

When I asked how this happened, she told me she didn't know but not to question it. "Just pack up and be ready to go." I didn't even have time for my wife to send me clothes, which is the usual protocol, so I would be wearing gray sweatpants and a sweatshirt. But I had no problem with that at all; I was going home!

The next five days were full. I spent time with the guys, encouraging them to remain connected to the Lord, and seeking God's heart. I continued my prayer walks, standing in the gap, interceding for so many guys I had big hopes for.

And there was lots of food. I could not believe how many guys cooked for me.

More than usual showed up at the Bible studies, and the final Sunday message was for me to share. It was such a blessing and honor.

Of course, there was one guy who had to test me. I am sure his plan was to get me to fight so I would not be able to leave. He was the leader of the Muslim group in my building and had stayed away from me the entire time I was there—although he talked about me to others often. For obvious reasons, he didn't like me much. One afternoon, two days before my discharge date, he ran into me and then challenged me, saying I ran into him. It was a petty thing, but he was seventy-two years old and had been in prison for fifty-four years of his life. So nothing about this behavior surprised me. He was institutionalized. And his Muslim faith left no room for Jesus in his heart.

I remained confident in God's protection, as I had for eight months. I stood up to him, made it clear I believed he was not going to hit me, and then he threatened me and walked away. I was shocked when two guys came up to me and offered to "take care of him" for me if I wanted. Of course, I said no and, instead, prayed for him.

13

MY FAMILY'S HEART

"For my thoughts are not your thoughts,
neither are your ways my ways,"
declares the Lord.
"As the heavens are higher than the earth,
so are my ways higher than your ways
and my thoughts than your thoughts.
As the rain and the snow come down from heaven,
and do not return to it
without watering the earth
and making it bud and flourish,
so that it yields seed for the sower
and bread for the eater,
so is my word that goes out from my mouth:
It will not return to me empty,
but will accomplish what I desire
and achieve the purpose for which I sent it.

You will go out in joy
and be led forth in peace;
the mountains and hills
will burst into song before you,
and all the trees of the field
will clap their hands.
Instead of the thornbush will grow the juniper,
and instead of briers the myrtle will grow.
This will be for the Lord's renown,
For an everlasting sign,
that will endure forever" (Isaiah 55:8–13).

From Shannon

When my husband was sentenced to twenty-four months in federal prison, the Lord immediately brought that verse from Isaiah to my heart. He wanted to assure me this was in His hands, and as wrong as it was in my mind, my heart had peace that we would see His will be done if we trusted Him. By faith we call it done.

Watching how God worked in my husband's heart and in my boys, how He provided for us in ways that were beyond anything we could imagine, and the mature relationship our family has with Him today is wonderful. We are grateful to Him and humbled He chose us.

We often hear stories about the political weaponization of the federal justice agencies but never imagine we will become victims of that treatment. Then it happened to us. As horrible as it was, we never doubted God's plan would work out to be the best for us in the long run. Despite this targeted attack, Mike never took his eyes off Jesus. He, of course, got upset over what was happening but had a peace that I admired. He kept saying, "God will handle this."

I believed God had called him for this, and he would be in "covert operations" for God, to not only reveal how desperately we need criminal justice reform in our country, but also to reach lost men in prison who would find hope and peace through a relationship with Jesus, a Savior they had not known before meeting Mike. What God did in and through Mike during those eight months was amazing. Mike often says as tough as it was being away from us, he would not pass up what he was able to do to glorify God.

Mike's life verse today is Genesis 50:20, which says, "You intended to harm me, but God intended it for good to accomplish what is now happening, the saving of many lives."

Today, as I watch Mike honor God every day with his life, there is no doubt lives are being transformed through his faith. We are grateful because God took us through this season in the deep valley, but He walked through every step with us. We will never forget the pain as it is always for His purpose in our lives.

This is not the end of the story but just the beginning. It's the beginning of all Mike will reveal about what happens behind bars and all God did there. God's glory is everywhere, even in the darkest places.

From Dominic (16 years old)...

"The hardest part . . . the first day we dropped him off was rough. The car ride home was silent for the entire hour and ten minutes. Daniel cried most of the way. My mom, I could tell, was hiding her emotions as well as she could. And for me, well, I was trying my best not to cry. I wanted to do something that would keep my mind off of everything.

Once we arrived home, I went to my room and tried to prioritize things so I would always have something to do. We watched a movie with grandma and mom that night, then mom, Danny, and I went to bed in their bed.

Once we woke up, we were still quiet. We would talk here and there but nothing much. We discussed some things we needed to get done, like selling Dad's desk and getting him a new one, selling our toys, and getting my room organized. I read some of my book, and then we went to our friend's, the Browns, house. We have known each other for our entire lives. We sewed some stuffed animals, and I made a dog paw. This made me think, *I want a dog so bad!*

After that, the girls ended up coming to our house and spending the night. We watched *Zootopia*, and Meagan went down early, and Danny and Mikaela fell asleep. I finished the movie and went down to bed. I lay in bed thinking about a lot of things but mainly about my dad. What he was doing and how he was doing were big questions. I prayed he would come home soon and that I could see him soon, whether it was visiting him or even him coming home. I just wanted to hear his voice and see his face. Then I fell asleep."

That was what I wrote on the first day my dad left. The first heartbreaking day of the next eight-plus months to come.

Not having my dad here has affected everyone internally, yet as much as we work to hide it, the internal feelings, fears, and sense of loss we have shows externally too. So it's obvious how it has affected everyone, just not in the same way.

I never thought I would be one to show my emotions on the outside, and knowing what I know now, yes, that is a good thing. When I tried to suppress them, it made everything harder. I was so overcome with an internal anger but more outward sadness that it caused my entire life to change—especially when it came to social interactions.

I would normally call myself a pretty social person and love to make friends with everyone, but it was like I purposefully cut myself off from that part of my life, and it resulted in a kind of depressing state, which I did not realize was happening. I lost sight of the Lord and just kinda lived. I did what I needed to do to get through the day, without consulting with myself about what was really going on in my heart.

I did not realize until the eight months was coming to an end what the problem was. There was this crazy realization that happened where I finally concluded that God was truly using the circumstances my family was experiencing for a bigger purpose. You may think, "What purpose would that be? You and your family went through the hardest time of your lives?"

You would be right to say that, except, you're leaving out the most important detail. That detail is that God is greater than our disappointment. He is the Alpha and the Omega, the Beginning and the End. With these simple yet powerful names, we can see the all-authoritative sovereignty of God and how He uses what the devil means for evil for goodness, in His glory and for His glory.

Once I realized that God was in control, His peace surrounded me completely. If you had asked me how I was doing in the middle of the time my dad was in prison, I would have told you I had peace, but that would have been a lie that I told myself to get through the day.

It may be an interesting way to put it, but just as a baby takes about nine months to be born, I believe it was similar in the aspect that it was a rebirth for my family. *Refining* is a term I use quite a bit when referring to this season.

My father talks about how he would never trade this time for anything because of what God did through him and in him while he was away, and I would absolutely agree to that. This was a time of refining for my family, and those are the seasons we go through that mean the most, whether we liked them or not, because we know that God is gonna make good out of whatever it was that happened, no matter how bad it seemed. I would never trade the incredible lessons I learned for anything because without those lessons, I would not be the God-fearing young man I am today.

From Daniel (13 years old)...

The day I found out my dad would be going to prison was devastating. Even more so because it was for a crime he didn't commit. Then the day came. We drove him to the federal prison; I gave him a final hug goodbye, and I sat in the car crying as

I watched my dad disappear through the door. The drive home was even worse. So much was going through my head, questions to be exact. Questions like: "Why, God, did you do this?" and "Why, Jesus, did you take my father away from me?"

And that's when God touched my heart. He comforted me, saying: "My child, I am your Father! I have a plan and purpose through everything. Just watch!"

Just watch.

Those words stuck with me. After crying the whole way home I went to my room, fell on my knees, and argued with God. Even after He told me everything was going to be OK, I still continued to argue and be frustrated with my heavenly Father.

I changed, that first month my dad was away. Angry, non-responsive to my God. But at school, I shielded it. I hid behind a brick wall and put all of my emotions away. My friends could tell that every day, I was becoming just a little more depressed. Until, one day, when my dad could finally call us.

He still had a smile, he still had that shine through the phone that I thought would never come out of him in such a terrible place like that. Right then, I had a real smile again, too, for the first time in months. I saw Jesus again, through him, and then I knew the enemy had taken my heart, burned it in his fire, and threw the ash in a dark hole.

But my God is the God of miracles. He brought me out of the shadowy pit the devil had put me in, gave life to my heart and spirit, and renewed me by the blood of Jesus. My life radically changed after speaking with my dad, and I walked in faith, knowing my father was changing lives in prison. That he was there for an amazing purpose. The fact is, my dad saved men, some who will be in there for the rest of their lives. Because of my dad, they have hope! They have something to look forward to every day after waking up and reading the gospel. They know the Creator of the universe still loves them, despite the crimes they committed. And now, because of God working through my dad, they will spend eternity with Jesus Christ.

I had given up there in the beginning, blaming God for everything. But later, I learned to walk boldly, stronger in my faith, knowing no matter the size of the giant, we can all still stand strong, become like David, and make our giants crumble to the ground. God is bigger than any worldly trials—remember that when you face your giants. God works through everyone, and Him working through my dad has changed my whole family's lives.

God told me to just watch. I kept those words with me, and now that I have watched His glory prevail over the darkness, I see that our God is greater than anything else.

14

HOME

The rain came down, the streams rose, and the winds
blew and beat against that house; yet it did not fall,
because it had its foundation on the rock
(Matthew 7:25).

Finally, April 8 arrived, and I was ready to go. I processed out, and when the guard drove me to the train station, he said he had been in the Bureau of Prisons for twenty-four years and never seen anyone have the impact I did in that building, bringing the presence and peace of God like I did. I told him it wasn't me; it was Jesus who lived in me, and the glory of the impact he witnessed goes only to Him. His opening gave me a chance to talk to him about Jesus for the entire drive to the train station.

My wife knew I was coming home, but we wanted to surprise our boys. We planned for her to take them out to dinner at Waterside in Norfolk. Then the plan was to drive toward the train station as if she had gotten turned around and didn't mean to go that way. I would be there waiting and could surprise them.

Of course, the best paid plans rely on others to make them happen, and the train was over an hour late, so she was forced to spill the beans before I arrived. But that didn't dampen the celebration when I finally arrived. It was so beautiful. I could not believe I was actually hugging my wife and boys again. We could not stop praising Jesus. The only sad part was I had to report to a local halfway house for processing and registration. I had been told by the prison staff that they would register me and likely send me home that night. I would have to go back in for orientation but could sleep at home.

That did not happen. (Spinning me again…)

The halfway house operates just like the prison but for profit. There is one person in charge, and they get paid big bucks to keep you there. They get paid less if you go home. So guess what happened? After an hour with my family, I had to say goodbye again.

My wife had made a doctor's appointment for me for the next morning, and thankfully, the decision-maker at the halfway house permitted me to go. That would become a critical decision.

The doctor saw my tonsil and heard the story about how it had been swollen for eighteen days now and gave me a strong antibiotic and referred me to the ear-nose-throat (ENT) specialists at Eastern Virginia Medical School. I scheduled an appointment for within three days.

When I went in, the doctor took one look and said in a direct and matter-of-fact way, "That's cancer. It has to come out now." *What?* My heart leaped into my already swollen throat, and it was hard to take a breath. I felt as if I'd been slapped across the face.

I had just "busted out" of the worst place anyone could live and now, was learning I had cancer! He knew it was cancer without doing any tests and scheduled the surgery for the following week.

I asked the halfway house leadership if I could be released to my house to recover from the surgery. The doctor had told me a tonsillectomy in an adult my age is one of the most painful recoveries of any surgery. My family and I thought surely the halfway house would let me go home. They know they have no staff or means to care for someone immediately after surgery, right?

They knew all that but still said no. Again, I was shocked at the inhumane treatment of a non-violent inmate who had only been down eight months. Every other man and woman there had served six to twenty-five years. I wasn't expecting special treatment but had expected some measure of humanity and common sense.

I had four days to convince the judge to write an order to override the decision of the "for-profit halfway house," a place that simply wanted me to remember that I am still under the thumb of the Bureau of Prisons and that they are in charge. I filed an emergency motion with the judge *pro se*, which means "without representation by counsel," and you won't believe it, but she sent it to my former public defender who had been "so much help" in the past.

That certainly wasn't necessary. Pro se motions are processed and heard all of the time. I continued to wonder if there was any way at all to get a fair shot in the justice system. Once the attorney got involved, she had two options: file an emergency expedited motion, which would be heard right away, or file normally, which she decided was appropriate. Not only did she not like me very much after I sent that judge the letter a year earlier, but she gave the prosecutor a call to get his guidance too. I can say that because of the horrible response he wrote.

The prosecutor had thirty days to respond. Of course, my safety, health, and comfort did not matter. Decency for another human did not matter. The risk of poor care, resulting in an infection, did not matter.

So I had the surgery and went back to the halfway house. For five days, I could not swallow anything except popsicles; I had to take liquid narcotic pain medicine that, while it burned going down, gave me some relief. I laid in my bed alone, with no help or support. It was miserable. Not once did anyone who worked there ask me how I was feeling, if I was OK, or if I needed anything.

As my doctor expected, the lab work on the tonsil revealed a cancerous tumor. Next up was a PET scan, which is a full body scan to check for other tumors. The test came back negative for any more cancer—praise Jesus!

My doctors scheduled me to begin immediate radiation on my throat for six weeks, along with chemotherapy to kill any cells disturbed during the surgery. They told me I would need a feeding tube in my stomach about the third week and could swallow nothing from weeks two through twelve (or longer). "The inability to swallow could be permanent," they warned me, "And hearing loss at some level is guaranteed." I'd likely lose bottom teeth too.

The doctor also told me that if I refused treatment, I would likely be back in six months with untreatable cancer in my lungs and bones and have less than one year to live. He knew I was in a halfway house and said there was no way I could go through this procedure without adequate care.

The woman at the halfway house had done nothing to help me after the initial surgery, and if you read the anger in the prosecutor's objection to my release from the house to home confinement for better care, it may make you sick, like it did me. After lots of prayer with my wife, I rejected the radiation and chemotherapy. There was no way I could commit to that treatment and be in the halfway house. I did everything I could to get through the red tape, to have the judge make a different decision about this, to talking to the Bureau of Prisons and halfway house leadership. They all gave me the same response. They were not concerned about my treatments nor my need for proper care, which they could not provide (admittedly), and didn't care when I told them I would reject the treatment and the possible outcome of doing that.

I wonder what makes people who have families and loved ones of their own, who take an oath to serve and protect and provide care for other people, become perpetrators in such a broken system, tossing their personal values and character out the window?

I felt comfortable, believing God would protect me since the federal authorities would not. I believed God brought me out of the prison early so we could discover the cancer, and I would be healed in Jesus's name. The entire struggle also revealed the need for a review of public defender-prosecutor relationships and of how prosecutors control everything. None of my experience was about justice. I was targeted as I tried to take matters into my own hands, upsetting that prosecutor who controlled not only my freedom, but my well-being.

The good news was, I was able to leave daily to work in ministry for a church leadership firm. I could have lunch with my wife almost every day and watch my kids at their games on some days. I focused on getting my life back in order, earning money, and seeing my family as often as I could.

By late June, I had weekend passes to go home, which was nice. Spending time with my family was all I cared about. I was seeing a neurosurgeon for the cervical spine problems and getting physical therapy, injections, and the treatment for the spasms helped me feel much better. The numbness had dissipated significantly, and my dizziness was not as frequent.

I went home for good on July 31 (over three months after being released from prison), wearing an ankle bracelet. I didn't care—I was home! I was still under the supervision of the halfway house but had met with my probation officer. It was like a breath of fresh air talking to him. I could tell in my first brief conversation, he was going to be fair and treat me with dignity. Finally, I had encountered a government employee who cared. I knew I had to do my part—follow the rules—I have been a rule follower for most of my life. But I learned it wouldn't be easy.

The supervision from July 31 to September 16, when I would finally be released on probation, was difficult. The rules and limits are very restrictive. What I couldn't understand was why a minimum security, white-collar "criminal," who served eight months of time, was treated the same as a murderer who served twenty-five years.

September 16 arrived like Christmas, and my ankle bracelet was removed as I was transferred from supervision to probation.

The next day, I met the guy who would oversee me for the next three years, Brian Williams (who gave me permission to use his name). You hear stories about probation being tough, where officers are looking for people to make one misstep, so they can send them back to prison. About six in ten (62 percent) of the prisoners released across thirty-four states in 2012 were arrested within three years. The recidivism rate at the federal level is 71 percent five years out,[5] and that number is largely blamed (anecdotally) on the reputation of probation officers who are overworked and seeking ways to reduce their workload. Thankfully, that was not the situation in my case. God knew what He was doing. I have always believed He puts us together with people in life for His Kingdom purposes, and I believe He knew I had been through enough. Brian was firm in his explanation of the rules, rules established by the court, but he was also fair. I liked him as a person and respected him in the role he had. I could now work full time and travel. I could finally get back to my life.

15

FAITH

---

*You intended to harm me, but God intended it for
good to accomplish what is now being done, the
saving of many lives* (Genesis 50:20).

Just as I grew busy, working in real estate sales and in ministry,
speaking at men's groups and churches about all I had been
through and how amazing God is, I woke up one morning
with a couple of swollen lymph nodes in my neck. My stomach
fell, but I remained resolute in my faith.

I got in to see my doctor the following day, and a nee-
dle biopsy revealed tumors in both lymph nodes. The doctor described it as "a very aggressive cancer" because it had
returned so fast. Immediate major surgery called a radical neck
dissection was scheduled for four days later.

What was so good about the timing of this was that I had been through so much, I had already fully surrendered to God, and I trusted Him completely. I felt like He had something more for me to learn and to do through this newest challenge. The doctors were surprised at how calm and at peace I was, so right then, I took the opportunity to give God the glory.

Now, I had to tell my family.

My wife handled it with the faith she always displays, by trusting God completely and believing in her heart He was in control. We agreed He still had a lot for me to do for many years to come. And in that assurance, we rested.

My boys had been through so much already and were on a real high having me back, involved in their lives and school and sports and our prayer times, with the reinstitution of Friday night pizza and movie nights, so this was tough for them to hear. We prayed together and believed God would take care of this, just like He had conquered everything else for the past year or so.

Our family loves God, and we will always seek His will for our lives. That was never more evident than when we talked about what we were facing at this point. My boys were twelve and fifteen, and because of the year before, mature beyond their years, especially in Christ.

One of my son's first comments after I told them was, "We pray for His will. We claim His sovereignty, and today we have to stand on that." Oh, we shed some tears, and while we felt some fear, we sought His comforting embrace in the situations that we couldn't understand or explain.

When I checked in for surgery on that Friday, we were told I would be in the hospital at least three to five days, and I prepared myself for a difficult recovery for the first day or so. The surgeon opened me up, removed fifty-two lymph nodes, and did a biopsy of tissue inside my throat. Everything went well, and surprisingly, when I woke up, although bandaged up with a drain tube, I felt great. I wasn't in any pain and felt full of energy, and I praised God. My wife brought me Chick-fil-A. The nurses told me there'd be no way I would feel like eating. Ha-ha! They didn't know me. Eating God's chicken was high on my list of recovery activities.

An occupational therapist came by a few hours after I woke up and told me I needed to walk out of the room and around the nurses' station before they could consider sending me home. I laughed and said, "Let's go." Then I got out of bed, took a nice walk around the nurses' station, spoke to everyone, and got back to my room. "So, can I go home?"

Everyone laughed and then said no. They didn't really think I'd be able to do that so quickly and were amazed at my energy. Again, I got the chance to talk about the healing power of Jesus.

Later that evening, one nurse came in, and we talked about faith and surrendering to God off and on for a couple of hours. She told me she had planned to call off that day but felt a strong "gut" feeling that she should come in after all. Now she knew why. She said meeting me allowed her to know what it meant to meet with Jesus in a way she had not experienced before. We talked, prayed, and cried, and I was left in awe—and so humbled—by how God orchestrated that conversation.

The next morning, the doctor strode in, and I asked her if I could go home.

"Yes, around eleven."

Again, I was in awe of the goodness of God.

A follow-up PET scan the following week revealed no cancer anywhere in my body. The surgeon told me the margins were very good around the tumors inside the lymph nodes but still recommended radiation and chemo for the same reasons as last time. I won't get into all of the details or reasons, but again, through lots of prayer, my wife and I decided not to go forward with the follow-up treatment. It is interesting how the "standard of care" works in medical care today. It feels like it's about insurance and money, and doctors are fairly restricted from offering their educated advice outside of the protocols, or standards of care, likely established by non-clinical people. In fact, the doctors who had pushed me to get further treatment, once I said no, told me they concurred and did not believe I needed it. How sad it is that medical professionals are strong-armed into pushing certain treatments that could radically change our qualities of life forever, even if they don't believe it is necessary, simply to comply with some risk management protocol.

As I write this today, I am one year cancer-free. I see my doctors at EVMS and Virginia Oncology every quarter and have continued to engage in amazing conversations about Jesus with so many who work in healthcare. I don't know why God allowed me to get cancer, but He is using me to reach some of those people with His love, grace, and goodness. I am so humbled that He has chosen me for this important work and I will always be obedient to those callings.

My life verse had always been Philippians 4:13, which says, "I can do all things through Christ who strengthens me," and I will always believe that, but for the rest of my life it will be Genesis 50:20, "You intended to harm me, but God intended it for good to accomplish what is now being done, the saving of many lives."

What I hope by writing this book is that it causes a fire to burn inside you, a fire that compels you to seek justice. And perhaps, one that might see the justice system transformed into what it was intended to be. I pray God will reveal to the world those who are good and speak truthfully, and also those who are corrupt and who lie. Incidentally, the motion I filed asking the Judge for early release from the halfway house was ignored for 14 months before I finally received it marked "moot" since I was free. The irony in that is, I filed another motion asking the Judge for permission to co-sign an auto loan because my wife went to work and needed a car and of course the AUSA objected, and the Judge denied it, all within four hours. You really can't make this stuff up.

Most importantly, I hope you let this sink deep into your heart . . . with God, you can get through anything you are facing today, and you are never too far away from Him to be welcomed, even welcomed back. He stands at the door of your heart and knocks with His arms wide open, but you have to open the door. Once you do, you will find a peace and joy you've never experienced. God bless you.

ACKNOWLEDGMENTS

I want to thank Jesus for walking through a very difficult time in my life, which I could not have made it through without Him.

I thank David Hancock and his team at Morgan James for trusting me, working with me to get this work done, and believing in the importance of sharing this story and message of hope.

Also, many thanks to the friends who did not turn their backs on me, who believed me and showed their love to me and my family throughout my time in prison.

And finally, to my amazing wife, her parents, and my children, who stood by me, loved me, supported me, and never stopped believing in me.

ABOUT THE AUTHOR

Michael Morisi worked in corporate business for thirty years, most recently as president of PEOPLExpress Airlines. He felt called by God into full-time ministry following his work with the airline and has spent the past seven years serving the Lord. Today, he is a pastor and coach who points those he meets to Jesus. Michael lives in Suffolk, Virginia, with his wife Shannon and two sons. He also has a grown son who lives in Los Angeles.

Endnotes

1 Wikipedia. United States incarceration rate, accessed September 20, 2022, https://en.wikipedia.org/wiki/United_States_incarceration_rate.

2 [not original case article] Olivia Jaquith. "Not Guilty, Sentenced to Life: Attorney for 'Waverly Two' Submits Appeal in Virginia Supreme Court" Nextstar Media Inc. Channel 8 ABC News, Richmond, August 18, 2022, accessed September 29, 2022, https://www.wric.com/news/taking-action/not-guilty-sentenced-to-life-attorney-for-waverly-two-submits-appeal-in-virginia-supreme-court/.

3 The Marshall Project, accessed September 25, 2022, https://www.themarshallproject.org/2020/11/04/the-truth-about-trials.

4 H. Michael Steinberg Website, accessed September 27, 2022, https://www.hmichaelsteinberg.com/if-you-are-charged-with-a-federal-crime.html.

5 Matthew R. Durose; Leonardo Antenangeli, PhD. "Recidivism of Prisoners Released in 34 States in 2012: A 5-Year Follow-Up Period (2012–2017)." Bureau of Justice Statistics (BJS). July 2021, accessed September 26, 2022, https://bjs.ojp.gov/library/publications/recidivism-prisoners-released-34-states-2012-5-year-follow-period-2012-2017.

A free ebook edition is available with the purchase of this book.

To claim your free ebook edition:
1. Visit MorganJamesBOGO.com
2. Sign your name CLEARLY in the space
3. Complete the form and submit a photo of the entire copyright page
4. You or your friend can download the ebook to your preferred device

Morgan James BOGO™

A **FREE** ebook edition is available for you or a friend with the purchase of this print book.

CLEARLY SIGN YOUR NAME ABOVE

Instructions to claim your free ebook edition:
1. Visit MorganJamesBOGO.com
2. Sign your name CLEARLY in the space above
3. Complete the form and submit a photo of this entire page
4. You or your friend can download the ebook to your preferred device

Print & Digital Together Forever.

Snap a photo

Free ebook

Read anywhere